CHICKEN SOUP FOR THE TEEN SOUL

CHICKEN SOUP
FOR THE
TEEN SOUL

Real-Life Stories by Real Teens

Jack Canfield
Mark Victor Hansen
Stephanie H. Meyer
John Meyer

SCHOLASTIC INC.
New York Toronto London Auckland Sydney
Mexico City New Delhi Hong Kong Buenos Aires

The following pieces were originally published by the Young Authors Foundation (© 1989–2007) in *The 21st Century/Teen Ink* magazine. We gratefully acknowledge the many individuals who granted us permission to reprint the cited material.

Losing Tyler. Reprinted by permission of Lisa Gauches. ©1999 Lisa Gauches.

Bargaining with God. Reprinted by permission of Kelly Powell. ©1996 Kelly Powell.

Knowing When. Reprinted by permission of Meredith Caine. ©2000 Meredith Caine.

The Old Puzzle. Reprinted by permission of Emily Russell Newick. ©1996 Emily Russell Newick.

So Over You. Reprinted by permission of Sharlyne Gan. ©2004 Sharlyne Gan.

(Continued on page 317)

ISBN-13: 978-0-545-07227-4
ISBN-10: 0-545-07227-1

12 11 10 9 8 7 6 5 4 3 2 1   8 9 10 11 12 13/0

Printed in the U.S.A.   23

First Scholastic printing, January 2008

Cover design by Larissa Hise Henoch
Inside formatting by Dawn Von Strolley Grove

We dedicate this book
to the 450,000 teenagers who have
submitted their work to us,
making *Teen Ink* magazine and TeenInk.com
possible during the past eighteen years.

Contents

1. LIFE STORIES

2. FRIENDSHIP

3. FACING CHALLENGES

4. LOVE STORIES

5. PERSONAL HURDLES

6. FAMILY STUFF

7. THROUGH THE GENERATIONS

8. FITTING IN

9. MONUMENTAL MOMENTS

Foreword

Most teen books are written in retrospect by those who say, "Hey, I remember what I felt like when I was sixteen —the arguments with parents, flunking math, and falling in love. I remember the day my best friend decided he didn't want to be my best friend anymore." It's not unusual for used-to-be-teens turned authors to sit down and write their stories.

This book is different. It isn't a collection of adults reinventing their teen years. It isn't a scrapbook of the past or a touched-up picture of teen life cut and pasted into something it wasn't.

This book is, instead, those restless years close-up, personal, and in progress. The stories were written by teenagers during their teenage years. This book brims with the stuff of everyday teen life, the thoughts and worries and dreams and insecurities and fantasies and hopes, not of someone looking back, but of someone looking forward. *Chicken Soup for the Teen Soul: Real Stories by Real Teens* is a collection of stories and poetry that is different because it is written from the trenches of youth.

Within these pages, its voices are like the teens themselves: all over the map. Some are soft and sad; others are loud and strident. They're bright with hope and tinged with fear. They're the voices of kids shouting at a rally, kids answering a question in class, and kids whispering in the back of a room.

Unlike some collections, nothing is pat here. It isn't a collection of teenagers standing in a row, all wearing the same white shirts and sunny smiles. Here are braces and frowns, dress shirts and T-shirts, earrings and nose rings, thirteen and nineteen, standing side by side.

It is *Chicken Soup for the Teen Soul*—teens speaking out about being a teen today.

Beverly Beckham

Beverly Beckham is a columnist for *The Boston Globe* and is a frequent contributor to the Chicken Soup for the Soul series. She is also the author of *Gift of Time* and *Back Then*.

Acknowledgments

We wish to express our heartfelt gratitude to the following people who helped make this book possible.

Our families, who have been chicken soup for our souls!

Jack's family: Inga, Travis, Riley, Christopher, Oran, and Kyle, for all their love and support.

Mark's family: Patty, Elisabeth, and Melanie Hansen, for once again sharing and lovingly supporting us in creating another book.

Stephanie and John's family: Alison and Rob, our children, who have been a continuing source of encouragement ever since the beginning of *Teen Ink* magazine in 1989 when they were just teenagers themselves. They, and now their families, have helped guide us every step of the way.

Our publisher, Peter Vegso, for his vision and commitment to bringing Chicken Soup for the Soul to the world.

Patty Aubery and Russ Kalmaski, for being there on every step of the journey, with love, laughter, and endless creativity.

D'ette Corona, for being there to answer any questions along the way.

Patty Hansen, for her thorough and competent handling of the legal and licensing aspects of the Chicken Soup for the Soul books. You are magnificent at the challenge!

Veronica Romero, Barbara LoMonaco, Teresa Collett,

Robin Yerian, Jesse Ianniello, Lauren Edelstein, Lisa Williams, Lauren Bray, Laurie Hartman, Patti Clement, Connie Simoni, Karen Schoenfeld, Marty Robinson, Patti Coffey, Pat Burns, Kristi Waite, and Blake Arce, who support Jack's and Mark's businesses with skill and love.

Michele Matriscini, Carol Rosenberg, Andrea Gold, Allison Janse, and Katheline St. Fort, our editors at Health Communications, Inc., for their devotion to excellence.

Tom Sand, Lori Golden, Kelly Johnson Maragni, Patricia McConnell, Kim Weiss, Paola Fernandez-Rana, the marketing, sales, and PR departments at Health Communications, Inc., for doing such an incredible job supporting our books.

Tom Sand, Claude Choquette, and Luc Jutras, who manage year after year to get our books translated into thirty-six languages around the world.

The art department at Health Communications, Inc., for their talent, creativity, and unrelenting patience in producing book covers and inside designs that capture the essence of Chicken Soup: Larissa Hise Henoch, Lawna Patterson Oldfield, Andrea Perrine Brower, Anthony Clausi, and Dawn Von Strolley Grove.

And to the *Teen Ink* group: a special thanks to Kate Dunlap Seamans, whose editorial expertise has been a mainstay of our organization for the past eight years; Katie Olsen, whose abilities and intellect have brought her to fill the enormous task of production/designer coordinator and web master; and Tara Jordan, who has been an invaluable part of creating this latest *Teen Ink* book, as well as managing every task necessary for our monthly magazine and website. Thanks also to our longtime volunteer, Barbara Field, who has been a support in so many ways through many years of service. In addition, we appreciate the extra effort from our ever-evolving team of high school and college interns, including most recently, Dorry Samuels and Emma Halwitz. We also deeply appreciate all the support of our extended staff: Larry Reed, Bob Kuchnicki, Ruth Cretella, and Tyler Ford.

Thank you to our extended family and friends who always helped and offered their support on many levels: all the Raisners (Barbara, Debra, Eli, Jason, David, and Amy), Joseph Rice III, Jennifer and Rick Geisman, Katherine Brinson, Lowell and Paula Fox, Denise Peck and Paul Chase, Ann Oliveira and Jef Mcallister, Leana Arain, Barbara Wand, Molly Dunn, and Zick Rubin.

And our even larger family of Foundation Board members: J. Robert Casey, Richard Freedberg, and David Anable, as well as our Advisory Board: Beverly Beckham, Michael Dukakis, Milton Lieberman, Harold Raynolds, and Susan Weld, who have served with us through the years.

In addition, we want to thank the teachers from over seventy-five high schools from thirty-seven states and their more than thirty-four hundred students who read and evaluated sample chapters of our *Teen Ink* books to give us their feedback and ratings that helped determine the final selections.

Thanks also for all the support from the following individuals who have allowed their voices to be heard through exclusive *Teen Ink* interviews that have appeared in the magazine: First Lady Laura Bush, Gen. Colin Powell, Sen. Hillary Clinton, Sen. John Glenn, Rev. Jesse Jackson, Caroline Kennedy, Sir James and Lady Jeanne Galway, Maya Angelou, George Lucas, Alicia Keys, Whoopi Goldberg, R. L. Stine, Ice Cube, Andrew Shue, Tony Hawk, Pedro Martinez, and Ira Glass.

Because of the size of this project, we may have left out the names of some people who contributed along the way. If so, we are sorry, but please know that we really do appreciate you very much.

We are truly grateful and love you all!

Introduction

Welcome to *Chicken Soup for the Teen Soul: Real Stories by Real Teens*. This is a unique book in that *Teen Ink* has collaborated with Chicken Soup to offer you stories from the *Teen Ink* magazine, book series, and TeenInk.com.

So, what is *Teen Ink*? Eighteen years ago, we founded a nonprofit organization to publish a magazine where everything was created *by* teens *for* teens. We started *Teen Ink* because we believed that every teen should have a chance to express their ideas, concerns, and creativity. And this philosophy lives on at *Teen Ink* today. Without any staff writers, we have always depended completely on our readers to fill the magazine with pieces that have power and meaning for teenagers everywhere. The magazine and website are read regularly by millions of teens around the world. At this point, we have published more than forty-five thousand teenagers in the pages of our magazine and on TeenInk.com. Each year we publish teens from every state and many foreign countries, and you, too, are invited to send us your work.

Now we are very excited to share these stories in this new book, where you will find universal experiences—from the tragic to the triumphant. You will read stories of pain and bewilderment, as well as tales of strength and inspiration.

Over the years, we've been touched by the passionate reactions to these stories from readers who have sent heartfelt letters and feedback that document how they, too, know just how Lisa felt when she went on her first date, or when Kevin lost his father. They have been there as well but never realized there were so many others who shared their feelings.

And isn't connecting what it's all about? What is more important than how we all relate, connect (and sometimes disconnect)? What is closer to the hearts of teens everywhere than family, friends, relationships, and experiences?

We hope that you and your friends enjoy these truly remarkable stories and poems. So flip through these pages and sample these amazing tales.

—*Stephanie and John Meyer*

Share with Us

We would love to hear your reactions to the stories in this book. Please let us know what your favorite stories were and how they affected you.

We also invite you to send us stories you would like to see published in future editions of Chicken Soup for the Soul. Please send submissions to: www.chickensoup.com.

Chicken Soup for the Soul
P.O. Box 30880
Santa Barbara, CA 93130
fax: 805-563-2945

We hope you enjoy reading this book as much as we enjoyed compiling and editing it.

1

LIFE STORIES

Love the moment. Flowers grow out of dark moments. Therefore, each moment is vital. It affects the whole. Life is a succession of such moments, and to live each is to succeed.

Corita Kent

Losing Tyler

Love does not consist in gazing at each other,
but in looking together in the same direction.

Antoine de Saint-Exupéry

To the observer, we appear to be two average high-school students. He pores over a college guide, and I write my college application essay. Chewing on the end of my no. 2 pencil, I'm trying to think of words to live by. That's my topic.

My mind wanders, and so does my gaze, away from the blank page. I watch Tyler. His forehead creases slightly, and I know in a few seconds he'll snap his head slightly to the side to get his hair out of his face. Counting down—three, two, one . . . His head tosses back slightly to the left. It's mere habit now, since he cut his hair short months ago.

I also predict in a few seconds he'll swear in Gaelic. He does, and I laugh. It's one of those situations where you know the other person better than you know yourself. And, lately, I have found myself observing him more and more.

The expression on his face probably mirrors my own, our eyes filled with stress, frustration, and bewilderment.

Where did the time go? Days seem to drag, but years pass quickly.

I rest my head in my hands and watch him. Words to live by still haven't come to me. I have known this person for twelve years. He's been my best friend since preschool; when I have a problem, I go right to him.

As I watch him, he coughs, and I worry. I almost ask him if he wants to go outside for some fresh air, but it was his idea to go to the library, so I say nothing. At first glance, he looks fine, perhaps a little tired. But I see the circles under his eyes and the holes he has punched in his belt because of the weight he's lost. That's the third new hole this month. Without looking up, he says, "Stop staring at me."

Without moving, I reply, "I'm not."

Once, when I was nine, I looked up cystic fibrosis in the dictionary: *a common hereditary disease that appears in early childhood, involving generalized disorder of the exocrine glands, and a deficiency of pancreatic enzymes.* As a nine-year-old, I was very confused. "That's not what Tyler has," I told my mother. "He coughs a lot and doesn't like to eat. The doctors must be wrong."

She just hugged me.

For almost as long as I can remember, Tyler has been sick. And it has always amazed me how positive he is. In turn, he's made me positive. I used to be convinced that a lung donor would show up, so sure the geneticists would find a miracle cure. But lately, as I watch him grow thinner and thinner, my positive feelings have turned into a facade, and I worry all the time.

I know he grows frustrated, too. Frustrated that he won't have the chance to do everything he wants to. Frustrated thinking he shouldn't go to college and waste his parents' money on an education he could die in the middle of.

Tyler's angry, too—at the world, at God, and, sometimes,

even at me. After all, I'll get to do things he won't. But he would never admit this. In fact, he hides it well. Only I, who have known him so long, know these things.

I'm angry, too, but for selfish reasons. Soon, I'll have no one to talk to. No one will ever understand me the same way; I'm losing the best friend anyone could ever have. God is taking back the kindest, gentlest person I'll ever have the privilege of knowing.

And I still have to think of words to live by.

I feel a tear slide down the right side of my face, but make no move to wipe it away. I don't want him to look up and see me crying. I'm usually good at keeping in my tears, but he always knows.

He looks up. With his left thumb, he wipes away the tear and smiles at me—the same smile he gave me twelve years ago when he offered half a peanut-butter-and-jelly sandwich to the little girl across the table who had forgotten her lunch.

Tyler looks at the top of my blank page to where I have scrawled "Words to Live By" and smiles again.

"Always remember, Lise, these words to live by: 'Our sincerest laughter with some pain is fraught'" [Percy B. Shelley].

Lisa Gauches

Bargaining with God

It takes a real storm in the average person's life to make him realize how much worrying he has done over squalls.

Bruce Barton

When I think of my family, I consider it "normal"—two working parents, a daughter, son, and even a white picket fence. Our family life was stable and dependable—until one January day.

It was a Sunday morning, and I was getting ready to babysit. My door was shut. Suddenly, I could hear my mom running up the stairs, screaming my name. I thought Dad must be playfully chasing her, as he often does. I opened the door to watch the fun. It might have been the tears in her eyes or her terrified look, but I knew something was really wrong. Soon, I was downstairs with my family, each with our own tears and terrified looks. My father was in the basement, seated in a chair, his limp body being supported by my brother. He could hardly talk; only murmurs came from his mouth. His eyes were squinted, and he was breathing heavily.

My mom sent me outside to "wait for the ambulance." I wasn't in any state to argue. In the two or three minutes it took for the medics to get there, my whole life changed. *What was happening? What would I do without my father? Why him? Why me? Why hadn't I told him I loved him more often?*

I could hear the sirens in the distance. They sounded light-years away.

When help finally arrived, I ran and begged them to hurry. The medics quickly went to my father and, after a quick examination, put him in the ambulance and rushed him to the hospital.

At the hospital, the hours dragged like years. Finally, the doctor came and told us what had happened. His medical jargon meant nothing to me, but I did catch the word "stroke" here and there. *My father, MY father, had a stroke? How could this be happening?*

My dad stayed at the hospital for two days. Both nights, I bargained with God. I knew that if there was ever a time when I needed his help, this was it. I swore that if he spared my father, I would never ask for anything again. I vowed never to take my father for granted again. I promised everything I had to have my father back. I wanted my crumbling world to be normal again.

I just hoped God was listening.

On the third day, the doctor met us as we were coming in. He said he had to talk to us. *This is it,* I thought.

He sat us down and started to talk. I did all I could do to concentrate on his words. Finally, I heard "fully recover." I burst into tears—at last—happy tears. My prayers had been answered. I had a father.

Since then, I realize that nothing is *ever* certain. Now, when my parents say something, I listen. When the family sits down to dinner, we enjoy each other's company. Dinnertime isn't just time to fill our stomachs; it's a time to fill our heads and hearts with memories to last forever. I have come to believe firmly that you don't realize what you have until it is almost taken away.

Kelly Powell

Knowing When

The minute you settle for less than you deserve, you get even less than you settled for.

Maureen Dowd

Tank tops, boxer shorts, newly designed hairdos, and faces painted with all the wrong shades of makeup: another Saturday-night slumber party with best friends. Julie, Molly, and I had been friends since Julie's mom forgot to pack her a snack the first day of fourth grade. Friends already, Molly and I agreed to share our half-eaten granola bars and chocolate milk with the new girl. None of us would ever have guessed that this act of kindness would lead to many potato-chip-filled, secret-sharing nights.

Tonight, however, was different. We were edgy and nervous, quick to snap at each other. The carefree makeup escapades were over as we each tried to look our best and ravaged Molly's bathroom for the perfect shade of eye shadow. I stepped back once to notice the chaos that engulfed us but was quickly snapped back as Julie snatched the mascara from my hand. Molly, realizing Julie now possessed the key to long, luscious lashes, quickly chased after her. I chuckled as I watched my two best friends run out the door.

Our playfulness had returned, and I joined in the wrestling match on the bed, the prize no longer mascara but the pure enjoyment of friendship. We were interrupted by the doorbell and shrieked with anticipation. *They're here!* I thought. Rolling off the bed, we pushed and shoved for a small corner of the mirror to check our hair and makeup. With the second ring, we cavorted down to the front door and anxiously waited for Molly to open it. She hesitated and looked at us uneasily. After all, we weren't just opening her front door, but a whole new era. Once this door was opened, there would be dating, holding hands, kissing, and heartbreak. The third ring reminded us that we couldn't back out now. Molly opened the door to three sweaty-palmed boys, obviously as nervous as we, and she invited them in.

Gathering in the living room, the three of us strategically placed ourselves around the table so that we were each next to the boy of our dreams. After sitting in silence for a minute, Molly offered drinks, and all three boys accepted, probably out of hope that it would spark conversation. Julie, Molly, and I glided toward the kitchen, attempting to look as graceful as possible but fell all over each other as we got there, babbling in hushed whispers about "our boys." Regaining composure, we stepped back into the spotlight and rejoined them at the table.

"Got any cards?"

"Um, yeah, just a minute," Molly said as she leaned over and reached in a desk drawer. "Here you are," she said, flashing a smile as she handed them over.

"Poker, anyone?" one of the boys suggested. The three of us shot glances at each other, knowing full well that none of us knew much about poker.

"Sure," Julie said, flashing a smile in her crush's direction. I looked at the boy sitting next to me and smiled at him, almost out of obligation. Picking up my cards, I looked at them with a blank stare, not sure how they could work together to mean anything.

"Hey," the boy next to me said, "look what I've got." Pulling a joint out of his pocket, he rolled it between his fingers, as though admiring a precious gem. "I stole it from my brother's room, but he won't notice. He has tons. Wanna try it?" He thrust it toward me. All I could do was look at it. I tried to say something, but when I opened my mouth, all that came out was air.

"Pass it this way," one of the other boys said. Lighting it, he took a puff and passed it to Julie. Nervously, she took it and inhaled. Not knowing what to expect, she inhaled too much and ended up coughing.

"Here, let me try," Molly said, grabbing the joint from Julie.

"All right, but let's play," one of the boys said, retrieving his cards from the table. Everyone else followed his lead and picked up their cards. Molly put the joint to her lips, inhaled, and coughed just as Julie had. The boy between us laughed as he picked up the joint after Molly dropped it and took a puff himself. Next it was my turn. A hundred excuses and reasons ran through my mind. Focused on my cards, the red and black became a blur. I laid my cards face down on the table.

"I fold." Getting up, I grabbed my coat. It was their turn to watch me walk out the door.

Meredith Caine

"Can't you tell this isn't my scene?"

The Old Puzzle

You are never too old to set another goal or to dream a new dream.

Les Brown

"I want to stay in my own house in Maine. Please don't make me go to Florida," my grandmother, Nanu, argued from her bed. It was 7:30 in the morning. My father had just explained that they were going to leave for Florida, where she lives in the winter. Dad reassured her that she loved the friendly people and warm weather.

Sitting in bed, looking both defiant and nervous, Nanu defended her position. If she stayed in Maine, she would be near her family; they wouldn't have to travel. Her friend Sally could move in and live with her. If the weather was bad, she would just hole up. She was thoughtful and logical, presenting a formidable argument for staying. But it was not possible.

Nanu has Alzheimer's disease, which has wiped away her short-term memory. She doesn't recall that she has spent the last six winters in Florida until she arrives and sees her friends, which causes her to be reluctant to leave

Maine. She reiterated, "I do not want to go to Florida. I do not know where I am going. I do not know anyone there."

My dad patiently convinced her that he would go with her and that she would enjoy Florida. It is painful to listen to Nanu describe her desire to stay in Maine. It is her home. She has no memory of Florida, so naturally she is scared about going there. There is no easy method of conveying to Nanu that she will be okay.

During a lull in the conversation, Nanu suddenly said, "What are we arguing about?"

My father smiled and said, "I was explaining that you need to get up so we can catch a plane to Florida."

Nanu replied, "Which side of the argument was I on?" Instantly recognizing the absurdity of her question, she leaned back in laughter. Humor in an awkward situation has become a frequent occurrence with Nanu: she will forget something and wind up laughing.

When I was young, my grandmother was active and energetic. Our biggest concern was keeping her in one place for more than thirty minutes. In the past five years, her memory has progressively deteriorated. She cannot remember what you just told her, where she left her purse, or whom you just introduced to her. She has acquired new habits that mystify the family, including squirreling away things in the back of closets and under beds, or taking everything out of a kitchen cabinet and placing it on the counter. She becomes frustrated when she realizes her memory problem inhibits her. Simple daily occurrences, such as losing her purse, epitomize the metamorphosis that has occurred.

I, too, have been transformed from the child I was to the person I am now. I wear dresses without crying or arguing. I do not suck my thumb, and I travel without my blanket. Nanu and I have reversed roles. When I was young, Nanu was the "adult," the "authority," taking my sister and me to the beach, to the Goldenrod for ice cream, to feed the ducks, and unfortunately, on occasion, to try on dresses. Nanu would present us with birthday presents that would excite us for weeks, like the spacesuits she bought one year. But now I take her on an afternoon drive or go to lunch with her at the Goldenrod. In reality, she is now the child.

It is painful to watch her become incapacitated. She has lost her independence. Nanu can remember her past abilities but cannot perform them. It is hard for her to realize that she must rely on others.

Although at times it seems like Nanu has lost everything because of Alzheimer's, I realize that she is still very much alive. It is easy to become depressed and think back when life was easier for her. I need to be patient and forgiving. Nanu will ask me the same question five times during one meal, and each time I will honestly respond. It is no help to tell her, "I just told you that." After the question is repeated many times, it is tempting to become frustrated, but I cannot. I must remember what Nanu has taught me: a positive attitude, patience, and an eagerness to unselfishly help others.

A mind afflicted with Alzheimer's is like an old puzzle. Over the years, we have fit the pieces together to form a clear picture. Every detail is in its proper place; every piece fits. As time goes by, some of those pieces break. Later, pieces are lost, which makes the puzzle harder to keep together. Yet, the shapes are still here, and we can see what the picture was. But, as more and more of the pieces are lost, the puzzle's picture becomes harder to decipher. Finally, the picture is gone. The rate at which the pieces will disappear is a mystery. Sometimes, lost pieces can be found for a while before they become lost again. There is no way of knowing how long the picture will last—a week, a month, a year, many years.

Nanu's memory is a mystery to me. Although she is no longer the adult she once was, she continues to teach me. She still thinks logically and, like many with Alzheimer's, her long-term memory is a treasure. She has never given up. She displays a positive outlook with humor as her ally. Her fascination with education, technology, and travel have been passed to each of her grandchildren. I hope that I can keep the puzzle for a long time. However, I know that there comes a time when the puzzle has too many missing pieces, and the picture fades.

Emily Newick

So Over You

Steam was rising from the hot black tar
As I was making my long trek home
On the last, first day of high school.

Thinking and walking gave me a headache
Like I was suddenly incapable of
Doing two things at once.

I walked past your house,
Like you walked past me in the halls.

The way you pretend you don't see me.
It makes me sick to my stomach.
Like stepping off a spinning carnival ride.

I try to block out the year before,
And all I can think of is how quickly you forget,
As easy as pressing the backspace on your keyboard.

So I walked past your house,
Like you walked past me in the halls.

Sharlyne Gan

I Sat with Nikki

*Never try to reason the prejudice out of a man.
It was not reasoned into him, and cannot be
reasoned out.*

Sydney Smith

Over the years, one thought has haunted me: *Why did
others think I was a sellout?* A few years ago, I was a new student at another high school. I made it my duty to observe
my surroundings and the people to see where I could fit into
this ecosystem. Immediately, I noticed something peculiar. I
realized how segregated it was. During lunch, the tables
were either predominantly white or black. Nothing like this
occurred at my previous school. Everyone mingled. But
when I sat with a white student during lunch, the defama-
tion of my character began. My choice of whom I sat with
affected the black population. They called me a "sellout."
The more I thought about the black students' reaction, the
more it bothered me. All because I sat with Nikki.

Nikki and I were both new. We were in the same grade;
we had a class together. She was very nice, and we immediately became good friends. I realized we shared the

same values. The only problem was that Nikki was white, and I was black. This was a taboo with the black population. They taunted me. No black person talked to me. People would stare and tell me that I did not know where I came from. When they heard the argot-type lingo absent from my speech, they ignored me—all because I sat with Nikki.

I experienced animosity from the black students many times that year. Once there was a group of students standing outside school. They found a way to segregate themselves once again. The whites were on one side and the blacks on the other. Nikki was sitting on the "white side" where she always sat because that was the ledge she found comfortable. She waited for her stepfather to take us home.

As I approached the double doors, I noticed a group of black students. I summoned my courage to go over to my white friend by saying to myself, *I do not care. I am going to do what I want to do.* I was relieved not to hear gasps or see stares. Instead, I heard clapping hands as they continued playing their game. However, I realized later that the situation had yet to reach its climax. The conversation turned to chocolate. They talked about white chocolate, and how white chocolate was still black. Another incident happened when I entered the lunchroom. Three guys said, "There goes an Oreo—black on the outside but white on the inside." I mustered up all my courage not to cry. All this happened because I sat with Nikki.

I tried to socialize with the black students, but only resistance greeted me. First, I tried talking to them in my classes where there was a maximum of two black kids in a class of twenty-five. They did not address me. However, one day I did happen to talk to one black girl because the teacher paired us together. She invited me to sit with her and her friends during lunch. She said she hated seeing me sit with "them." Her friends all looked at me as if I was from another planet. Their facial expressions said, "So, and who asked you?" When my new friend sat down, one of the others derided me by saying, "Angie, this is Micaela," in the same tone that I introduced myself. Her friends giggled. They said nothing to me during the entire lunch period while I tried to engage them in conversation. However, from their response it was obvious that my input did not interest them. This all happened because I sat with a white girl named Nikki.

I do not understand. A person would never believe that I experienced this today, rather than in 1963. The media inundates us with materials urging us to take steps toward equality and to promote racial harmony. Am I the only one who listens? Did the train pass every black person at this school? Why are we going backward? Did Martin Luther King and Malcolm X die for things to go back to the way it used to be, or worse? This is not 1963, when the prejudice occurs from the opposite side of the spectrum, but, today, the prejudice comes from my own people. They did not even know me! I do not understand. They made me an outsider—all because I sat with Nikki.

Micaela Golding

A Little Memorial

Only love and death change all things.

Kahlil Gibran

The sun beat down through the window onto my neck. I was sitting in my car seat in the back of our station wagon while Mom drove. The air smelled exactly like the foul odor coming from the truck in front of us, creating more smoke than a pile of burning tires. I don't remember what song played on the radio, but it was definitely a golden oldie since that was all my parents listened to. They cringed at the noise that came from the '80s and weren't too pleased with whatever the '90s had produced, either.

I was staring out the window, watching the white lines pass, when I noticed three small wooden crosses on a hill.

"Mommy, why are those there?" I asked, pointing my finger.

"Why are what, where?"

"Those, there," I repeated, but this time she looked in the mirror to see where I was pointing.

"That's a memorial." When she realized her young son

wouldn't understand that answer, she continued, "Some people died in an accident at that spot, so their family put those crosses there to remember them."

"Oh," I said, but I wasn't finished thinking yet. After a minute, a worrisome thought entered my head as Mom was turning onto a cloverleaf on-ramp and my shoulder pressed against the door.

"Mommy, I don't want you to die," I cried. "And I don't want to die."

"Don't worry, honey," she said, chuckling. "We're not going to die for a long, long time...."

* * *

Five days after my fourteenth birthday, at 10:00 on a Thursday night, my dad told my brother and me to go upstairs and get some rest. Sitting next to my mother, who slept on the couch, he said if anything happened, he would wake us up. I looked at her and watched her chest. I waited. I waited some more. I started getting nervous. Then, finally, her chest rose as she inhaled oxygen through the tube in her nose. I breathed in relief, said good night, and went upstairs.

Lying with my eyes open, I saw nothing. I heard my mom wake up. I heard bits and pieces of what she was saying to my dad. The words floated through the house, drifting to my ear, but I knew they weren't meant for me, so I shut my door. I closed my eyes tighter, as if this would further muffle the sounds, already softer than the beating of my heart.

Somehow, sleep overtook me. Maybe it was from exhaustion, the exhaustion that had accumulated during the last few years, and especially the last four months, as minerals accumulate in hard water on the white shower wall, turning it orange. These orange stains of exhaustion temporarily covered the white wall of worry and pain, dulling the blinding brightness and making it tolerable.

I knew I was awake from the pressure on my shoulder. My eyes were still closed, but the pressure tightened. I recognized the weight as a hand. Was it mine? I twitched each of my index fingers. No, I opened my eyes to look at the hand, and it was Dad's.

Light from the hall spilled through my door, illuminating one side of his face, but the pain was clear. I understood why he was standing there. He released a huge sigh and said nothing. He didn't need to. Soon, I found myself downstairs, sitting on my heels by the sofa. I watched her chest. I waited. I waited some more. Nothing. Not now. Not ever.

* * *

On the morning of my fourteenth Christmas, one present seemed to stand out. It was tiny, and I guessed it was jewelry. *Why would I want to wear jewelry?* I wondered. I put it aside and left it until all the other ones were opened.

Finally, I lifted the lid, and something gold gleamed inside. It was a cross.

It's not wooden, and it doesn't stand on a hill by the highway; it's better. Every time I inhale, I feel a slight pressure on my chest, and I am reminded of my mother. Every now and then, someone will point at the end of my chain and ask, "What's that?"

And I will say, "That's a little memorial. . . ."

Jason Jellies

Control

My head starts to spin and my eyes begin to hurt as I stand up. Looking briefly at what I ate for dinner before I flush gives me a sense of control. I have been doing this for more than a year now, and I have never felt better—or worse.

I feel better because I feel more in control of my body, like I'm deciding what food does to me, not the other way around. I know my trigger foods, and I know what I can eat without feeling guilty. There are few of these. I eat breakfast so I don't get migraines, and at lunch (if I eat anything) it's a plate of tomatoes with salt and pepper or macaroni and cheese, which doesn't stay in my stomach long. Cake at dinner is a staple, as is bread and rice and whatever else I feel like eating, mixed with a lot of milk to help it come up. One of the stalls in the faculty, staff, and guest bathroom has a thick door that locks and a window so that I can see during the day without having to turn on the light and the fan and not hear someone coming in. It's harder to do it at night, but I have learned which times are easiest.

I know that there are others, even though we don't talk, especially about food. We are not friends. Whoever said "It takes one to know one" wasn't kidding. You can recognize the white spots on their teeth and the redness in their eyes, and you know you're looking at your reflection. Often these girls are the best—at school, sports, music, dance, whatever—and always appear very strong, a useful facade for keeping a secret.

Before I quit, I had told only one person, a best friend. When she asked how I stayed so skinny, I didn't want to say something obnoxious like "I can eat whatever I want and not gain an ounce." So I told her. She didn't judge me. She wasn't eating much either, so she understood.

I had a few close calls. A roommate whose sister was like me confronted me after noticing my body wither during swim practice, but I told her that swimming two hours a day would make anyone thin. She knew I was lying, but we left it at that. Another roommate walked in on me once, and I just told her I was sick. She didn't think twice. Once we were at Denny's, and I guess I had been gone a long time because, when I got back to the table, everyone was joking about how I had been puking in the bathroom. I just laughed along.

It's hard to do it. First of all, it hurts. But you have to distance yourself from people for it to work. You can't let anyone come to the bathroom with you, which is contrary to female instinct, and you can't talk about anything serious, since you don't want to slip and tell. You let a few people get close, and that's it. Restaurants are easy because they have single bathrooms with doors that lock and loud fans. I used to go to a restaurant with my dad and get turkey, mashed potatoes, macaroni and cheese, cornbread, and root beer, and have a great time. He had no idea, mostly because I am so "strong" and "independent." I guess that's why everyone was so shocked when I told them. My then-boyfriend freaked out, believing it was his fault, and thought it wasn't cool to have a girlfriend with a "problem."

My friends and my mother were totally shocked when I

told them. My mother was half the reason I did it. She had gone to my school but was much thinner than me. She often reminded me, saying, "When I was your age, I was a lot thinner than you are" or "You're not skinny, you know" or "Have you put on some weight?" when I hadn't. I think she was jealous of my strength and intelligence, two qualities she did not have at my age. Maybe she tried to make me feel bad that I lacked her strong points: her physique and her social activity.

It also gives you a bad feeling when your friends are skinnier than you. You always size people up, girls more than boys, because you constantly have to know where you stand in relation to them. If they look better, you have no control over the unconscious hate that invades your consciousness.

I had to tell the school administration so they would let me stay home for the few days I needed to quit. I hated them knowing and talking about me in faculty meetings as the girl with the "eating issues." I didn't like for them to know anything about me, my body, or my real life. I had to go through counseling with this woman I grew to like. Another student was also seeing her since she specialized in our problem, so that student and I had a silent understanding, even though we didn't speak and weren't friends.

It's funny (well, maybe not funny, exactly, but interesting) to look back at what I put myself through. I have a picture of Kate Moss on my wall that says in big black marker: YOU ARE NOT MY IDOL. But that's a lie. I don't want to be her or look like her, but you can't help but know that she symbolizes what I am supposed to be. This impossible standard of slenderness makes many things challenging. It's hard to concentrate on schoolwork, hard to love, hard to let people love you, because you think all the time, "How could he/she love me? I'm so fat and heinous and disgusting and stupid. How could anyone want me?"

Even though I haven't done it in three months, there isn't one day I don't think about doing it. I have come close many times but have succeeded in resisting. Sort of. I don't look at it as a success; the hardest thing to say is "I know I'm beautiful even in this short skirt, and everyone knows it, including me."

Even now, with my incredibly wonderful, supportive boyfriend, I feel gross sometimes. He really does love me the way I am. I believe him, and he has helped me a lot. I'm moving, slowly. I work out, and I eat the best I can, treating myself to potato chips or jelly beans or nachos every once in a while, but it seems the less I care about what I eat, the less it can do to me. Maybe someday the fist ruling my world will be not one of iron, but one of my own.

Gulielma Fager

I Knew a Boy

One day, I met a boy. He had long hair, and he wore it down like an angel.

"My name is Rob," he said.

"My name is Anna," I answered, and then we smiled.

Rob was my best friend. We talked about heaven and love and coffee with just enough sugar and cream. Ours was a fairy-tale dreamland with perfect moments where we never ran out of things to say.

"Let's be hippies today," he said, and we donned our handkerchiefs and sunglasses, let down our hair, and talked of peace and love.

"Let's be bad," I said, and we scowled, decked out in black, and rocked to heavy metal.

"Let's be optimistic," he said, and we walked around in yellow, on top of the world.

"Let's be individuals," he said, and we made up puzzling outfits, contemplated anarchy, and laughed. This was our favorite game.

Sometimes we sang, sometimes we ran, sometimes we talked, but mostly we laughed. We had summers of perfection and idyllic winters. We had sunshine, and we had red cheeks, and we danced in the rain. It was beautiful.

"Let's be in love," I said, and I bit my nails and cried, afraid he wouldn't like this game. He danced.

"I love you!" he said, and on went our fairy-tale dreamland. But my stomach was upset, and my eyes cried without me at night, and I knew that it was wrong.

"Let's break up," I said, and he cried. And I cried for his broken heart and the way he didn't look at me anymore.

"I don't like this game," he said.

Then our fairy-tale dreamland disappeared, and we looked around to see where the colors had gone, and why our world was gray.

"I think it left with the love," I said, and I cried.

"But it was just a game," he said, laughing quietly, and I remembered that there were no kisses. My heart hurt, and I cried because I didn't realize the truth.

Once I knew a boy. Now he has forgotten our fairy-tale dreamland, and I watch him as his heart grows cold. He says that he is truly bad.

"Let's hate each other," he said, and I agreed. Then my stomach turned again, and I cried in the dark, and I knew it was wrong.

"Let's make up," I said, and we pretended. Then we tried to remember our fairy-tale dreamland, but he could not find the way, and I lost him.

"Let's say I've fallen in love with someone else," he said, and I smiled sadly because it was no longer a game, and he would never play with me again.

"Let's move on," I said.

I remember a boy. We once had a fairy-tale dreamland. Sometimes I still go there, looking for him, because he was lost.

"Let's be hippies today," I call, but I get no answer.

Once, I knew a boy.

Anna Holmquist

Our Masterpiece

A brother is a friend given by nature.

Jean Baptiste Legouve

It was huge. No, huge isn't even the word. Enormous? Perhaps. At any rate, it stretched halfway down the beach. Dubbed "Our Masterpiece," it was just that. My brother and I had spent the entire morning and half the afternoon working on our creation, taking only enough time off to dash into the water now and again. But it was worth it.

Turrets of sand towered high above the shoreline, their tiny seaweed flags fluttering in the gentle August breeze. An intricate labyrinth of roadwork weaved its way between the buildings we had constructed with a shovel, pail, and an occasional rude word. It was a bonding experience, my brother and I working side by side in the warm sun, exchanging fewer than ten spoken words but sharing our souls at the same time. I don't think I've ever felt as close to my brother as I did that day on the beach.

He was leaving for college the next day. Maybe that's why I felt such an urgent need to have one last hour with him. He was moving on to the real world, while I was left behind, still living out my little dream-filled existence.

"Darrell," I said as we sat back on our heels and admired our hard work. "Are things going to be the same when you come back? You've never left the house for more than a few days before. How are things going to be when you come home?"

He was silent for a minute. The chilly ocean spray began to creep slowly up the shoreline, advancing steadily toward the castle we had fabricated to hide ourselves. The sky was tinged a reddish purple, changing the ocean spray from blue to scarlet.

"Darrell?"

The water was lapping at the base of the sandy walls, licking away our foundation, intent on destroying the rest of our little world.

"Nothing ever stays the same," he said softly, and we began to pack our belongings.

Walking down the beach again, toward civilization, we looked back and saw the waves spilling over the tops of the turrets, changing everything, making our own creation unrecognizable.

Everything does change, I admitted softly to myself as I watched the water fill our footprints and wash them away.

Kerri Morrone

"Heads, I'm your best friend. Tails, it's Willie."

Five Minutes

Ever has it been that love knows not its own depth until the hour of separation.

Kahlil Gibran

It was 7:05. Not 7:00. Five minutes late . . . 300 seconds too late. The line at KFC for chicken. Waiting. Chicken. Five minutes. We arrived at 7:05 with a two-liter bottle of pop and soggy bags from the heat of the chicken. We were late. Searching the parking lot for an empty space. Going in circles. We were five minutes late. Three sisters late and unwarned.

We were two steps away from her room when a nurse greeted us with a smile and pleasant conversation. There we stood, two steps away in that hallway, smiling until the nurse realized who we were and who the chicken and soda were for. She took an awkward breath and asked if our aunt had called us. We told her no.

Then she began to say "sorry," but the throbbing in my throat deadened my hearing, and the thoughts inside me began to destroy my mind. It was not true. It couldn't be. We were only five minutes late. I knew what was coming.

Before she could finish, the soda had thudded to the floor, along with the food, causing a flood of mashed potatoes and gravy beneath our feet.

Releasing it all and grabbing hold of me, my sister was as unsteady as my grandmother the day she drank too many beers. There I stood in that endless hallway with loss-stricken voices echoing off every closed door. I stood with my sisters, but feeling so alone; reality caught me off guard and convinced me that I was motherless. I felt the change, but it did not change me. She was still my mother; I was still her daughter, just five minutes late.

Set the timer for five minutes, and in that five minutes, see what it does to you. Loss at 6:59 was nothing more than losing a quarter. As I stood there in that hallway at 7:05, loss was at the core of my world. Time had the upper hand.

Jill Telford

What Doesn't Matter

What doesn't matter is how I dress—
With granny pants and big, baggy shirts.
What doesn't matter is how I look—
With no makeup to mar the true beauty of my face.
What doesn't matter is how I talk—
With shy and quiet words.
What doesn't matter is how I think—
With never-before-thought-of ideas.
What doesn't matter is what people may say of me—
With people forever gossiping.
What doesn't matter is what people think of me—
Because I already know what I think of myself.
But what does matter is . . .
What I say, what I think, what I do.
What matters is . . .
What I believe, what I love, what I hate.
What matters is . . .
What I know, what I want to know, how I act.
What matters is . . .
Not what other people think or do or say,
But what I have done . . .
To make the world I live in be a place
    worthy of life and living.

Clara Nguyen

2

FRIENDSHIP

A friend drops their plans when you're in
trouble, shares joy in your accomplishments, feels sad when you're in pain. A
friend encourages your dreams and offers
advice—but when you don't follow it, they
still respect and love you.

Doris W. Helmering

Safe for the Night

A friend loves at all times.

Proverbs 17:17

"By my calculations, there aren't enough pills in the box." James' voice was low and flat. I was terrified. How should I respond to that? He sighed, and I knew I had to say something or risk having him grow cold again.

"James . . ." I struggled. "James, don't say that. I'm here for you, always, you know that. Please don't say that. . . ." I fought to keep my voice even and hide the fact that I was about to burst into tears. "Please . . . as clichéd as this sounds, that's not the answer." Neither of us could say the word "suicide."

"Manders, I know. You're . . ." He paused, and I could picture him sitting on his front steps, bundled in his coat at 2:00 AM, baring his soul over the phone. "You're my closest friend, my best friend, and I don't consider many people . . . if anyone . . . my friend. You're special, hon. But right now . . . it really seems like my best option."

I cried silently as I listened to him in so much agony. I could hear him breathing as he thought of what to say next, and when he spoke, I could hear the pain.

"I hate to say this to you, Manders. But you don't know how much I hate my life right now. I told my sister about this, and all she said was, 'That's selfish.' It's not, though. I used to think people who killed themselves were the weakest, most selfish people, but I was wrong. It takes an incredible amount of strength to go through with it." He sighed again. I pictured him staring up at the cold, winter sky, wishing for a way out.

"James, it's a permanent solution to a temporary problem." I could hear the strain in my voice, and I knew he could tell I was crying. "What happens if you do it and fail? Then what? And what if you actually succeed?"

Two hours later I woke up, the phone still cradled against my ear.

"James?" There was a minute of silence before I heard movement on the other end.

"Manders? What time is it? You sound like you just got beaten up."

"Gee, thanks. You don't sound much better. It's four. We fell asleep."

James chuckled softly, his amusement genuine.

"Hey, we slept together, in the loosest sense of the term. I guess we should hang up then, huh. We have school in what . . . four hours?"

I laughed, "Yeah, talk to you tomorrow. Think happy thoughts for me?"

"Silly Manders—I will. Cross my heart. G'night."

"Good night, James."

I sighed as I hung up the phone. I'd kept James safe for another night, but I couldn't make him happy. We'd known each other for five years. At least he trusted me enough to talk to me. At least he trusted me, period. I stayed curled up on the couch, thinking back to when James and I had first met. We'd talked on the phone for three years, and knew each other's deepest, darkest secrets. When he was a junior and I a sophomore, we discovered we both volunteered at the Haunted Graveyard and decided it was time we met. From that day on, we were inseparable. We talked on the phone every night, and when James got his license, we went to the movies together. Much to my dismay, his work schedule and the distance between our towns made it almost impossible to see each other more than once every few months.

When the school year rolled around again, James made it a point to stop at my school to see me. Without a car, I was forced to take the bus. James waited patiently in the parking lot, and I'd scamper to his car for a hug and a few minutes together. I looked forward to those morning hugs more than anything. At 6'3", James towered over me. I barely came to his shoulders. In his arms, I felt safe and warm, as if nothing could hurt me. If I was having a bad morning, just seeing him would calm me, and a hug would keep me happy all day. I loved him.

I realized that night that maturity comes not simply from growing older and wandering through life, but from life's harder lessons—lessons that come in the form of a tall boy, a bit too thin, who learned to trust, one step at a time. A boy who taught me more about myself, life, and pain than anyone before or since. And I knew, at that moment, that James would be okay, that I'd see him in the morning. I'd kept him safe—at least for the night.

Amanda Hager

Torrie, Jay, and Me

There are three things that grow more precious with age: old wood to burn, old books to read, and old friends to enjoy.

Henry Ford

"Do you want to go on the seesaw? I bet you haven't done that in years."

Fragments of light glistened through the black abyss, the moon providing just enough to make everything glow. A bitter wind swept through me. It was hard to believe gleeful children had occupied this playground earlier that day. Everything seemed utterly lifeless.

Lifeless. . . . The word echoed through my mind.

Don't die, Torrie, not now.

What the heck, I thought, following Jay across the school yard toward the seesaws. My feet sank deep into the pebbles. There was something very nostalgic about the moment, as if I were six years old again.

Jay held his end of the seesaw steady so I could get on. He mounted the other end and situated himself so he almost looked distinguished, but that only lasted a moment. Our weight difference caused me to fly upward, and Jay landed on the ground with a thud.

"That was classic. Where's a camera when you need one?" I joked.

Jay pushed off the ground, and I gradually floated back down. Unexpectedly, I began drifting upward again. I looked at the ground that should have been under my feet, but now there was just air. Jay's legs were too long, or maybe mine were too short. Nothing about that moment seemed real. I almost forgot why I was even there with Jay. He wanted to cheer me up, to take my mind off the accident.

I'm sorry I didn't keep in touch with you, Torrie. What happened? We swore we wouldn't drift apart. We never should have had that fight. . . .

Jay could tell I was thinking about her again. "Wanna go on the swings?" His voice cut through my silent wondering. I woke up.

Wake up, Torrie. All you have to do is show a sign that you're okay, I pleaded silently.

"I'd love to. When you were little, did you ever have a contest to—"

"—see who could swing the highest?" we spoke in unison. My laughter trailed off.

I wonder if you remember, Torrie. I always used to win. Well, not always. And now you're lying in a hospital not knowing if you'll ever walk again.

I forced myself to smile and continue the conversation. The swing was higher off the ground than I remembered.

"I bet I can go higher than you," he said. I shook my head. Leave it to Jay to turn a childhood pastime into a challenge. I rhythmically pumped my swing, and my hair blew around my face as I sailed through the air. I looked over at Jay. Although he had the same sparkle in his eye, and he threw me the same half-smile he always did, there was something different about him. Or maybe there was just something different about the way I saw him. The sparkle fell from his face and into the wind.

"Oh, Emily, smile."

I really wanted to, but it hurt to smile. I couldn't tell if the wind was burning my face or if it was a tear that rolled down my cheek.

We hopped off the swings and started to walk back toward his car.

"You know," he started, "you'll do so much better if you keep your mind busy with something else."

God, Torrie, why did you have to be so stupid? Why did you have to get in the car with someone who was drunk? You never even saw the curve in the road. The last thing you saw was the tree. . . .

"I'm sorry. What did you say?"

"Emily, let's talk. You want to know what ticks me off?"

"What?"

He almost didn't wait for my response.

"How the most beautiful girls hurt themselves for no reason."

I finally broke down, my blank stare welling up with tears.

"Come here."

I fell onto his shoulder. We stood there while he held me and let me cry. I finally realized what was so different about Jay: the sparkle in his eye was a tear I had never seen before.

"I want to fix the world so you never have to cry again," he said.

That night I cried for Torrie, and Jay cried for me.

Emily Carney

Leaning on Each Other

The breeze gently stirred the white curtains, filling my nose with the pungent aroma of a late summer afternoon.

Kate and I sat side by side, leaning against my parents' bed, watching TV, and occasionally talking. The pauses in our chatter were not filled with tension but rather a comfortable silence that happens between good friends.

A commercial that we both hated came on, so the silence was broken by our jokes and groans as we proceeded to make fun of the cartoon dancing across the screen. As the advertisement ended, the shrill ring of the telephone quieted us momentarily. I lunged for it.

Kate turned her attention back to the television but soon focused on me as my voice became less audible and my shoulders slumped forward.

I gripped the phone tightly, as if it were the one thing that would keep me from breaking down. My knuckles turned white. My breathing was shallow and came in little gasps as I tried desperately to consume the oxygen I had lost from holding my breath.

"Me, too," I murmured one last time before placing the phone in its cradle.

I felt Katie's arm tentatively touch my shoulder. I

squeezed my eyes tight, trying to get control and not let the tears that were so close to the surface overtake me.

Kate moved so we were face to face and embraced me. I clung to her for support as the tears were unleashed. We stood that way for five minutes before she gently stepped back to look at me.

"What happened?" Although her voice was soft, it boomed in the silence.

"My dad was admitted to the hospital. They don't know what's wrong, but it has to do with his heart." My voice was shaking, but I made no effort to steady it.

By some unspoken understanding, we sat back down to watch TV, leaning against each other for support instead of the bed. The shadows of the evening no longer seemed refreshing; they spoke of dark things hiding and waiting to be released.

I moved closer to Katie, grateful for her presence on such a cold summer's day.

Rebecca Bodfish

"We've been through a lot together,
including a lot of drive-thrus."

P.S. Never Forget Me

The loss of a friend is like that of a limb; time may heal the anguish of the wound, but the loss cannot be repaired.

Robert Southey

Ten days till Christmas. There's no snow yet, which is unusual. Last year, we had snow days the first week of November. That snowball fight we had at Katie's house is still fresh in my mind. I suppose I still owe you a white-wash. It doesn't seem fair that the year I'm a senior (the year we don't have to make up snow days) is the mildest winter yet. The grass is still green, and my cat is out chasing crunchy, fallen leaves. I've been listening to the *Les Miserables* soundtrack and humming Christmas carols all morning.

Ten days till Christmas. I wonder how your family is doing. They moved, and the house is still for sale. No one wants to buy the house upon whose steps you sat, gave out Halloween candy, teased your brother, yelled your hellos and good-byes to passing friends, and watched the trains rumble like steel thunder through your yard. The trains still go by, but I've stopped taking your street on my way home from school. Now I walk the tracks. You grew up and away with those tracks, and they bring a quiet solitude of comfort until the trains chug diligently back to present another dozen memorial shrieks for you.

Ten days till Christmas, but on that day it was two hundred and eighty-three. I was in the Upward Bound office at school, eating lunch with Erik and Andrew. I savored every bite of that pepperoni pizza, totally devoid of the mushrooms and olives you loved. Pulling, stretching cheese, smiley faces from the pepperoni and bacon, tossing your sausage and catching it in your mouth, you played with your food, like a six-year-old. You never did stop being six at heart, never did stop playing.

In the office, we shivered from laughter and the chill that crept through the windows. "I'm telling you," Andrew stated with mock seriousness, "Dasani is evil. There's little brain-sucking microchips in there that'll turn us all to drones." I laughed, nearly spitting out my pizza. Then, before my laughter died away, Cari came in looking as though the world had crashed in on her. Joe asked what was wrong. "My friend," she said numbly, "committed suicide. Justin Bies."

All I could think was, *I know that name. I know that name.* My world crashed, imploded, died with Cari's. I suppose that's what shock is: to be stuck on one thought—*I know that name. O, Lord God, I know that name*—unable to compute any other data. There is something terrible and real about not having to search to put a face to this name. I didn't have to wonder if he was the quiet kid who sat in the corner of my history class two years ago. This name, this person, this fellow human being, who lived and breathed the day before, this young man, my first crush, one of my closest friends, who signed my yearbook with a flourish, was dead. For good. Forever. . . . The bell rang. *I miss you already. . . .*

I obediently went to French class, stumbling along with the crowd. I was blind and deaf to the world, but inside I was raw with awareness. Entering the classroom, I was still numb, and there was Reena. My friend. Our friend. We hugged, and I felt swallowed up in your absence. Reena and I have always been each other's comforter and counselor. When Jake was killed in the car accident, when Mr. Dunkelberger was taken by an aneurysm, the teachers tried to explain everything away, but, in the end, Reena was the one I leaned on. Class started. Mademoiselle Stutzman, teary-eyed, read the notice. Her voice shook, and she read the same form that was always read:

We regret to inform you that
Such and such
Died at this time in that place.
Counselor offices are open if
Anyone needs to talk.
Blah, blah, blah.

I've practically got it memorized. I should. That was the fifth one. This time, though, my tears fell. I made no sound, but Mademoiselle Stutzman may have noticed a few miniature hills and valleys bearing witness to the tiny saltwater drops on my homework assignment. She didn't know you—though you would have liked her individuality—but her grief may have swelled in her heart when she corrected my *avoir* conjugation and gazed on the evidence of my sorrow. She'd have tucked her hair behind her ears in an attempt to stay clear and get on with things.

But we'll never get on with things, not totally. I felt then how deep the hole was that you left behind—deeper than the pond we waded through in seventh grade when I got that slug stuck to my glasses and you laughed so hard. Now I felt like I'd never laugh again, not with a heart so full of emptiness. Teachers and students alike spent the rest of the day doing their own thing to express our common grief—talking, thinking, or, in my case, madly scribbling in my diary.

Of course, I got the suicide talk from my parents. All those "It's not your faults" and "We'll never understand whys" reverberated in my brain. I cried in church that Sunday. I didn't mean to. The pastor was giving his usual you-never-know-if-you'll-die-today speech and used you as an example: "Just this week a teenager blew his brains out." You know how I've always hated such thoughts of violence. So graphic and ugly. I had to recount March 16 so many times, it became automatic. I found out at lunch. He shot himself. A shrug to say that that was all.

But it wasn't all. There's so much more I never told them. How Heather, Ray, Megan, you, and I ate lunch at the picnic table and had to chase the seagulls away from miserable cafeteria food—you always pointed out the gull with a hunched back, calling him the Godfather. How we threw a bagged dead snake at each other so many summers ago while playing a game that left us delirious with the fun and grossness—"Oh, my gosh, it's a dead, headless snake!" How we spent the hour in science passing notes, enlisting the help of those six rows between us, subtly reading and writing what Mr. White called a "hot note."

How you laughed, joy rolling and rollicking out from deep inside. The sound of your voice when you told a joke, happy and impatient, the punch line rolling off your tongue almost before the joke. Your duck-footed walk and serious clothes and perpetual mocking of each and every teacher.

Weeks passed, and the snow melted—for once without you begging for one more snow day—and spring sprang up everywhere. Months have gone by, and now you and your gelled hair and mischievous eyes are a memory. What once was sharp enough to prick blood is now a haunting ghost of a pain, softened by use and love, but conjuring no sweet Casper-like images. I still see your deep-brown closed casket in my mind's eye. There were so many flowers, flowers you would have picked out of boredom or ignored. I miss you, but the ache is gone. That desperate, lost feeling is displaced by a glance at your picture.

Did I tell you I got my braces off? I work at the library now, and I gave blood for the first time yesterday. I'm getting my driver's license in a few weeks, and in one month, I will be eighteen.

Meanwhile, there are only ten days till Christmas.

Stephanie Skaluba

Stop! LEGO Thief!

*A child becomes an adult when he realizes that
he has a right not only to be right but also to be
wrong.*

Thomas Szasz

I only need two more LEGO wheels, just two! Matt is
lucky that he has so many wheels. I wonder if he'd miss
just two tiny little gray and black wheels. I know it's
wrong to steal—my mommy taught me that—but I have
to finish my airplane. Perfect, Matt left the room. Here's
my chance. I did it. I took two LEGO wheels. I'm good. He
didn't even notice when he came back, but who could?
They were only two tiny LEGO wheels, and he has tons.

I went home with those LEGO wheels hiding in my
pink pants pocket. My parents wouldn't know; Matt
would never know; no one in the world knew but me. I
connected the new wheels to my plane. It looked awesome. I felt a little guilty because Matt was my best friend,
but at the same time, no one knew, so I would never be
caught. I planned on giving them back when I finished
using them, but then I forgot.

As the years passed, I had one of those "I want to be a kid again" moments and decided to unearth my bag of LEGOs from under my bed. I hadn't played with them since I lived in Alabama with Matt. I dumped the bag out on my bed and there they were—the LEGO wheels I had stolen. The word *stolen* penetrated my mind. How did I remember this? I can't even remember my homework assignments, let alone a couple of small toys.

I was a thief, a crook, a criminal. I was only five when I took them. Did I know better? Of course I did. My parents and Sunday school teachers taught me that it was wrong to steal. So I stared at the wheels with a burning desire to just throw them away and forget it had ever happened, but the guilt kept nagging at me.

Since I was the only one who knew, why did I feel so awful? I just had to get rid of this feeling of betrayal and dishonesty. To think that a five-year-old knew it was wrong just as a fifteen-year-old does shows that what we learn as children sticks with us.

I took out a piece of paper and wrote a letter to Matt. I hadn't talked to him in ten years. Confessing something like this felt a little silly. Maybe Matt would think it was funny and just laugh. I hoped he would think it's funny and laugh because I hear that Alabama is a big supporter of the death penalty. I sealed the envelope, but the letter still sits on my dresser. I never sent it. I'm almost sixteen, and I still can't face my fear, take responsibility for my crime, and send Matt what is rightfully his.

Can I use the excuse that I couldn't find his address? His dad was in the Coast Guard, so they moved a lot. I know that's a bad excuse. I can't live a dishonest life. I am disgusted with people who can't 'fess up to their crimes, who don't take responsibility for their actions.

Honesty. It's a word children learn at home, in church, at school, and yet no matter how many times it is drilled into our heads, it doesn't register with many. Someone does know of my crime spree, and that is God. And having God be disappointed in my actions doesn't make the problem any better. And yet knowing all this, the letter still sits on my dresser, and Matt still doesn't know he's missing two LEGO wheels. If anyone knows a guy named Matt who used to live in Alabama and had a friend named Patti, tell him I have a letter to send him, and I need his address.

Patti Hulett

Mirror Image

*Many people will walk in and out of your life.
But only true friends will leave footprints in your
heart.*

Eleanor Roosevelt

I have known her only a short while, but somehow I
know she is my friend. It is not the kind of friendship I've
had before—built on habit or fueled by fear and insecurity.
No, this is a friendship that, although new, feels as comfortable as a pair of old leather boots. Around her I am not
afraid to be myself, but rather I am unguarded. I tell her
everything, but it's as if she already knows. She knows
because it is also about her. She can truly understand what
is going on inside of me. She understands my life because
she is going through it, too. Both of us are venturing away
from what is considered normal, comfortable, and familiar
and are venturing toward the unknowns of adulthood and
independence. But with this new staunch independence,
we are glad we have each other to hold on to.

It is strange for me, though, to have this new support
because I am so used to going forward alone. It has

always seemed that no matter how close I got to another person, they never really understood how I felt. I knew this because none of my old friends shared my interests, and none were willing to try the things I enjoyed. I always ended up conforming to their needs and standards because I felt what I did was unimportant—until I met her.

When I look at her, I see myself looking back. Though her eyes are a different color, they see the world as mine do. The mouth may be a different shape, but it smiles at the same things mine does. Her ears are not the same, but they still delight in the same music. Her voice differs in pitch and intonation but says the things I cannot put into words. When my hands reach out looking for something to cling to, her hands catch mine and cling back, just as hard. She is my friend, my other self, my mirror image with a different face.

When I peer into the mirror, however, I do not see a carbon copy of myself. Her hands paint and draw, while mine write stories and essays. Her lips sing and play the harmonica, while mine just speak incessantly.

She wants to live beneath the ocean with the dolphins and orcas, but I want to spend my life among the stars in the sky. Still, together we make a solid image. It is as if, with the strokes of her paintbrushes, she fills in all the holes my words leave behind. Then she sets my words to music, writing the most expressive songs.

I am apprehensive about having a friend like her, though, because a friendship like this involves opening up, exposing my heart and mind and soul. Doing this means trusting the person, and with trust comes risk— risk of losing, of being rejected, of getting hurt. I know what it's like to be hurt, betrayed, and abandoned by a friend. But I think she is different. Of course, I have been wrong before. I have been sure that I've found a lifelong friend, a soul mate, only to discover that my heart had huge blinders on, and the "friend" actually was a foe. No matter how much I pretend I don't care, I am afraid of getting hurt again.

Above all, I don't want to be reduced to hiding behind a vacant smile, so as not to offend anyone. I don't want to have to pretend I'm someone I'm not just to make people happy. I hate the awful, closed-in feeling I get when I can't be myself. But I am myself around her, and she seems to like it. Still, out of habit probably, I sometimes catch myself guarding my words or actions around her. I know I can't do that if I want this to be a true friendship. But what if I'm wrong? What if she doesn't feel the same way? What if she's only putting up with me so as not to hurt my feelings? I've had these doubts before and have discovered they were well-founded.

Still, this time might be different. I must have faith in that. If I want this to work, I must open up. I must lay out my heart, mind, and ego, and truly believe that she won't stomp all over them. I must believe that, somewhere, someone is watching me and guiding me along. This must be true, because somehow in this great big universe of ours, somewhere between her sea and my sky, we found each other.

Meghan Heckman

"You didn't just tape something to my back, did you?"

I Closed My Eyes

*You get tragedy where the tree, instead of bend-
ing, breaks.*

Ludwig Wittgenstein

I closed my eyes. It was just another Monday, and I was
back in chemistry. Tim leaned over, pushed up his visor,
and made a face at me, rolling his eyes. It wasn't his
favorite subject, but he made an effort. He looked back at
me and swung his arm in a serving motion. We were both
ecstatic to be in first place in our badminton tournament.
I laughed and whispered, "Candy corn tournament, here
we come!"

I opened my eyes and stared at Mr. Miller's black shoes.
My hand was pressed against the cold window outside his
room. It was no longer Room 306; it had become his room,
and a place where I would sit and cry and hold his hands.
It was his room now.

Mr. Miller's shoes were black, like the ones my dad had.
The tip of his right shoe was no longer shiny, but scuffed
from hours of rubbing it against the other. He stood awk-
wardly, leaning on his right foot, as if trying to balance.

His laces were frayed, lying loose on the floor. I slowly dragged my hand down the window pane onto the black rubber trim. My fingertips traced the edges and made their way to the cold tile wall, searching for a crevice to hide. I felt torn apart. I closed my eyes and took a step around the corner.

As I moved, my mind closed to every thought, and yet, at the same time, I seemed to have millions of ideas surging through my brain.

Oh, God, I prayed, *if you would just please let him be all right. Just give me some of his pain, give a little of his pain to each of us, and make him all right. I promise I'll be nicer to people. I'll tell my friends and family I love them every time I see them. Oh, God, please.* Even as I heard these words in my head, I knew I sounded desperate. But it was only a second before I stood face to face with one of my worst fears.

Tim lay on the hospital bed, his eyes closed and his arms at his side. His orange visor was on the pillow next to him. His lacrosse stick balanced on the bedside table, tempting someone to pick it up and toss a ball around. A teddy bear with a blue bow was tucked under his right arm. A wide, dark blue tube in his mouth was taped to his lips. Countless other tubes emerged from his nose, arms, and legs. His chest rose and sank rhythmically with the sound from the machine that stood next to his bed. The teddy bear rose and fell with him.

I looked down through tear-filled eyes at one of my best friends. Slowly, I picked up his limp hand and locked my fingers through his. I shut my eyes, and every image I had of Tim flashed before me. I watched as my mind replayed the hours I had spent with him, the way he made me laugh and feel important. I saw him, smiling at me, and then laughing loudly. I opened my eyes. We were not going to the tournament together; I would have to go alone.

The doctors called it a "real tragedy," something that couldn't have been anticipated. They said his allergies had become much worse, and he hadn't realized it. It was as simple as that: his allergies were too strong. The priest said that he would always be with us, and whenever we missed him, we could just talk to him, and he'd hear us. Mr. Miller told us that Tim was alive in a sense because he saw a bit of Tim in each of us.

But these are just nice things that people say when others are sad. The truth is that Tim Miller, a sixteen-year-old athlete, comedian, son, older brother, and best friend, is gone from this world forever.

He was not saved that day, despite my efforts to bargain with God. It is hard to believe that almost a year has passed since I was with Tim that day.

Although I will never see him again, every time I close my eyes, I see him smiling, laughing. The pain he endured is gone, and even though I have an aching pain in my chest every time I think of him and wish he was here, I know he is with me. He is holding his lacrosse stick and teddy bear, wearing his orange visor, and encouraging me to do my best, to do everything that he never had a chance to do.

Annabel Murphy Schizas

Destroying the Bully

You cannot shake hands with a clenched fist.

Indira Gandhi

If intentionally hurting another soul is part of human nature, then it is a concept I will never fully understand. Many bullies do not take the time to think about those they are hurting, or about what goes on behind the closed doors of their victims' lives. One thing that I have happily discovered is that the ideal bully hates nothing more than if the victim is not shaken by attempts to harass and intimidate. A bully's reason for existing is to be mean, and it is a shock to receive kindness in response. A bully does not understand friendship, but it is one of the most important aspects of life. By spreading kindness you can make friends out of even the worst enemies.

I experienced one of the worst forms of bullying: sneaky bullying. Fortunately for my bully—let's call her Kristy— she was loved by adults who were easily fooled by her false compliments. I met Kristy the first day of art class. I loved art, but as excited as I was, Kristy quickly made me dread it.

When I entered that art room for the first time, I spotted the last open seat in the room and sat next to Kristy. Before I even had a chance to introduce myself, she looked at her friend and said, "Let's move." Assuming there must be something drastically wrong with the table, I followed. She looked at me oddly, and I assumed that it was because she didn't know who I was, so I politely said, "Hi, I'm Ann." She cracked a sly smile and replied, "Well, Ann, I'm Kristy, and my friend and I moved tables because we didn't want to be near you." That was the first snakebite.

For the next few days, I tried to avoid Kristy, but that only worked for a while. She began to poke fun at everything about me: my hair, what I wore, the way I talked, and how I created my art. I told my friends and family, and they offered some ideas like changing classes or talking to the school counselor, but even she loved Kristy. So I decided to attempt the impossible—I was going to make Kristy my friend.

"Kind words are short and easy to speak, but their echoes are truly endless," Mother Teresa once said, and I only wish I had known this when I first met Kristy because it would have made my solution much more obvious. I began to respond politely whenever Kristy threw a nasty comment my way. Instead of the silence or hurt face she expected, Kristy got a compliment thrown back at her. This inflamed her with more fury, and for a short time she criticized me even more, a sign that my plan was working. The conversation usually went something like this:

"Ann, I have to tell you, that is the ugliest picture I have ever seen. I mean, what is it? Another snakebite?"

"Well, Kristy, I think it's really beautiful, and this blue paint I am using reminds me of that pretty shirt you wore yesterday."

Eventually, my kind comments got to her, and she

asked, "What is with you, Ann? Why are you being so nice to me?"

I responded, "Well, because I want you to be nice to me." What happened next was amazing. It was like Kristy's whole world flipped upside-down. Even her friend looked shocked by my courageous statement. The snakebites would soon end.

For a few days, the three of us sat in silence during art class, but it was Kristy who made the next move, saying, "Ann, I really like your shirt. Where is it from?" After that, the next conversation was easier, and the one after that even seemed natural. Eventually, Kristy and I knew all about each other's lives and what boys we liked. I had destroyed the bully side of Kristy by making her my friend.

Kristy and I remained friends for a few years after our rough start and had some good times that led to even better memories. Although Kristy eventually moved away, she taught me a lot about myself and what matters most in life. Friendship and kindness are so important in life, and after my experience with Kristy, I know I will always have a friend no matter where I go, even if she at first appears to be a bully.

Ann Virgo

Emily, the Soccer Star

The love we give away is the only love we keep.

Elbert G. Hubbard

"BZZZZZZZZZ." The sound of my alarm clock was enough to make me jump. I turned over with a groan and stumbled out of bed. From the second my feet touched the carpet, I could tell today was going to be another scorcher. I pulled on my hospital pants and white T-shirt. Although I tried to eat, the butterflies in my stomach won the battle, and I settled for apple juice. Today, I would begin my summer job. I was volunteering at the hospital. When I had decided to work there I had been excited, but now I was very anxious about what I would be doing.

At the hospital I learned that most of my job would be to take patients to their rooms and to do other odd jobs. On Fridays, however, I would spend time in Pediatrics, visiting with a child. The first few days passed quickly. By Friday, I had forgotten about my date on the Pediatrics floor. So when I was instructed to go meet Emily, a leukemia patient, I tried to plaster a calm smile across my face, but inside I wanted to cry. Even with her lack of hair and an IV in her arm, she mustered the strength to smile and speak with me.

I soon learned that Emily was eight. She loved going to the beach and playing with dolls, and she had an older brother named Ryan. She was on the town soccer team and proudly informed me that she had scored more goals than anyone else on her team. With our incessant chatting, that first Friday very quickly came to an end.

When I told her I would be back in a week, she begged and pleaded for me to visit on Monday. I couldn't resist her toothless grin, and so I "pinkie-swore" to be back after the weekend. It wasn't long before I was spending lunch breaks with Emily and leaving the hospital long after my shift had ended to spend time with her in the game room.

On days she felt strong enough, we played soccer, even though it was not allowed. It was hilarious to see the nurses turning their heads away, pretending not to notice when Emily's infamous and most prized possession—her black and white soccer ball—would fly through the air. On rare occasions, her illness would get the best of her, and we couldn't play. On those days, I would read her favorite children's books to her or we would play Barbies on her hospital bed. On one occasion, we even cut off Barbie's hair so she could be Emily's twin.

I discovered many things that I admired about Emily. I was most impressed with her will to live. Not once did I see her shed a tear over the pain she must have been hiding behind those clear blue eyes. In addition, her constant optimism, along with her contagious laughter, made her unlike any eight-year-old I had ever met. She was wise beyond her years, and her incredible physical and emotional strength made her an inspiration.

Toward the middle of the summer, her "yuck days" (as she called them) began to outnumber her good ones. I can remember one particular day when I arrived at Emily's room to find her in an unusual state: she was quiet and in a deep sleep. After talking to her mother, I learned that Emily had been given her life "sentence"—she only had a couple of weeks left.

I went home that night with a pit in my stomach and a lump in my throat. I retreated to my room without dinner and cried for hours. I felt so helpless and would have given anything to take her pain away, but all I could do was hold her hand as she vomited from the medication being forced into her tiny body. Even more, I hated this disease that had wreaked havoc inside her and cut her life far too short. It was then that I decided to make the best of these weeks with Emily.

Even during her last few days, Emily brought joy into the lives of those around her. She laughed and giggled with everyone who visited, and she marveled at all the cards and stuffed animals she received.

One evening after dinner, we played soccer—a special occasion because it was something she hadn't had the strength to do in quite a while. Ending the night with her favorite book, Cinderella, I once again "pinkie-swore" I would be back the next day for another round of soccer. She gave me a the biggest hug that her frail body could muster.

The next day, I sprinted down the corridor to see my favorite patient but instead was greeted by her mother. Through her tears she told me that Emily had passed away earlier in the morning. Her mother told me how wonderful I had made Emily's last few months, but that didn't help ease my aching heart. Just as I was about to leave, her mother handed me an envelope with my name written in red crayon. I knew immediately it was Emily's handwriting because of the backward S scribbled across the front. Opening the envelope in the car, I found a drawing of us playing soccer. On the top was written "To my favorite soccer player." The tears that I so desperately tried to keep inside sprang from my eyes. At that moment, I realized I had been truly blessed by the presence of this amazing eight-year-old.

Even today when I start to forget, I take that folded drawing from my wallet, look at her tiny body, clad in that teddy-bear hospital gown, and smile back at that toothless grin that taught me about life, love, and friendship.

Suzanne Timmons

Friendly Training

*The companions of our childhood always pos-
sess a certain power over our minds which
hardly any later friend can obtain.*

Mary Shelley

*F-5, this is L-7. We seem to have encountered a bit of difficulty
in our maneuvering. Shift to gear two on three—1-2-3, quick,
shift! I've got you, change view, bear hard right, one start, now!
F-5, shift to gear four, gear four now! Shift, shift, quick, I'm losing
you; I'm losing you.*

In sixth grade, we invented this game. We had just
exited a movie theater on a "double date" with two of our
classmates. Instead of "girl talk" about which one was
cuter, we sat down at two arcade games, the car type with
seats. Neither of us wanted to spend two quarters on a
thirty-second game, so we decided to pretend we were
astronauts on a mission in outer space. The game occupied us while we waited for her mother.

We kept playing. Every time we hit a bowling alley,
arcade, or movie theater, we played. She was the only one
who knew how to play, and together we mastered outer

space. I thought I could always save her by shifting into a different gear, calling mission control, or hitting the quarter return button four times. It never occurred to me that I could really lose her.

We've gone to school together for twelve years, meeting in kindergarten. We made our First Communion together, and even made Confirmation side by side. She was the only girl with whom I could play tackle football (until I broke her nose), act out *The Lion King,* or give live telecasts from the middle of a severe hurricane, also known as her pool.

Our other friends don't know about my red boots in second grade, how she got sick on "Visit Your Pen Pal Day" in third grade, or how her fifth-grade map of Texas didn't have enough rivers. We were in the same Girl Scout troop and quit the same year. I was even her "doctor" during a tragic fall off the balance beam at our "Olympic Gymnastics Competition" in the woods. When she fell into a tree that ripped a deep cut in her leg, I bandaged it on the spot with duct tape and gauze. She still has the scar, and I'm pretty sure now that the cut deserved stitches.

We went on vacations, had sleepovers, took piano lessons, and did every project together, except the science fair in third grade when we both made a solar system. (Hers was obviously better, but I won because I dressed up like an astronaut. She retaliated in fourth grade with a killer project on weather systems, which surpassed my bird-feeding experiment.) We watched hockey and football games together, made each other Christmas and birthday presents, and even won the title "Best Friends" in our eighth-grade yearbook. We always said we would be friends forever, yet never admitted we were the other's best friend.

She almost moved away in sixth grade but didn't. We

almost went to different high schools but didn't. Those things just didn't happen to us. I thought I could do anything with her by my side. I thought we would go to school together forever. I thought we would always be best friends.

As high school began, we clung to each other, making the same friends and even having lockers near each other. I was lost when I learned we only had one class together. She didn't play soccer. I didn't play tennis. We made different basketball teams. I asked her to join the church youth group, but she didn't like it. She made other friends, and so did I, though we sat together at lunch and still hung out on weekends.

Sophomore year, we were lucky even to see each other during the school day. I went on a vacation with other friends, not her. We went to Florida with our softball team but weren't roommates. I rarely called her, and when I did, she wasn't home. My mom asked if we were still friends. I laughed and said of course we were. It never occurred to me we were growing apart.

During junior year, she found a new best friend. I'd call, and they would be at her house. I'd ask her to go out, and she'd say, "Sure, as long as she can come." They were together in school all the time, with the same classes and activities.

The hardest thing happened in English class. The teacher told us to write about a relationship. I didn't want to write about my best friend and instead wrote a simpler piece about my family. At lunch, classmates began asking about each other's topics. Her new best friend informed us that she was writing about her "new best friend." I was crushed.

I guess I never realized that my new friends probably made her feel neglected, and she probably never thought I felt the same. But there are so many things that only she and I share. Her new best friend does not know about our pretend brothers and sisters, where the best hiding spots in the church choir are, or how to play McDonald's with oddly shaped trees. I thought I had lost her, but in truth, reality had won. We aren't little girls who watch Disney movies together, but we can hold on to our memories.

No matter how alike we are, we're two very different people. I'm going to have to learn to let her go sometime, and the training has already begun.

F-5, this is L-7 reporting. If you shift back into two with a quick start, I won't lose you. I've got you; don't worry. I won't forget anything; I won't give you up; I'll never let you go.

Lisa Kelly

Dear Amy

The first duty of love is to listen.

Paul Tillich

In life, there are moments when we, as human beings living in a world that sometimes seems superficial, are touched by rays of hope. It's easy to forget that while society seems to be corrupt and we are struggling to become the best we can, there are good, unselfish people out there willing to give what they have to enrich the life of another.

Being an adolescent is perhaps one of the most insecure periods of life, but I was always more than just insecure. Riddled with low self-esteem but constantly trying to outdo myself, I was seldom proud and always reluctant to accept compliments. Sometimes, however, what I did surprised me with its courageousness, like that rainy Saturday afternoon when I wrote that letter I had been meaning to send for nine years.

Although many refuse to admit it, we all have idols. If I could remove small, incremental qualities from certain people—writers, singers, musicians, poets—and put them together to form myself, I would be satisfied with who I am. Perhaps by writing this letter I could achieve some aspect of those goals.

I wanted to know her secrets: why she was such a good lyricist; what made her so articulate and candid at times, but relentlessly private at others; how she could have survived the turmoil of the music business since the early seventies. While I wondered, I also respected her and appreciated her music. It was her words I could always relate to, her instrumentals that helped me to study. It was often frustrating because she was never a favorite with my friends. But they accepted my love of music regardless, and except for occasionally teasing me, they understood why I was moved by it.

Mailing the letter was perhaps one of the bravest things I have ever done. Not only did I tell her everything about myself, but I enclosed some of my most personal poems and watched fearfully as the mailman drove away, my dreams trapped in his truck. I knew I would most likely not hear from her, or at the very most, I expected some fan-club information, but what I received in the mail two weeks later shocked me and completely changed my outlook on life.

It was the kind of envelope that comes with personal stationery—small, with her return address stamped on the back. Tearing it open, I could only read the first line:

"Dear Amy . . ."

The words were jumbled together, and I realized that, not only had she acknowledged my letter, but she had written by hand to tell me I had touched her deeply, even though she was in the midst of promoting a brand-new album.

My poems were good, she said, but if I could be a bit looser, letting the creative side come forth, I would be better. She closed the letter with, "Let me know. . . . Love, Carly."

My first instinct was to follow her directions completely, writing freely whatever came into my mind. I immediately sent these thoughts to her, hoping for another response. I didn't realize what I was asking until I received another letter exactly one week later. She had not only torn through my thoughts, but rewritten them in a wonderfully poetic format, instructing me on how to improve, congratulating me for trying.

I think I became greedy. I wanted her to read everything I had ever written. I didn't realize how busy she was, and I again took advantage of her generosity by sending another poem, asking to be helped with her editing techniques. My perceptions were so cluttered; I hadn't taken the time to sit down and read what she had said as if she were a teacher and not a superstar singer/songwriter.

The third and final letter I received was much like the second: she had made so many corrections that her suggestions were written in the thin margins, taking up the entire page. She then went on to rewrite what I had written, giving me some of the best suggestions I had ever had. My disappointment followed when she explained that her editing had taken her an hour, and she would not have that kind of free time in the future, but she knew I was getting better, and I just needed to believe in myself.

"I know you can do it," she wrote, "you're going to be really good. . . . take these lessons, I hope you can learn from them on your own. . . . Love, Carly."

When the letters stopped, I sat down and read all of them over and over. When I could absorb what she had said, it all became clear to me. I wrote her a farewell thank-you letter and never heard from her again. Maybe her way of believing in me was not letting me become dependent on her and having more faith in myself. I'll never know how to thank her for such a wonderful realization.

Few people today would have done what she did.

During the three or four weeks we wrote letters, I admired her on talk shows and late-night shows, as well as television specials and radio programs, so I knew her time was scarce.

Soon after she wrote me, my name probably became a foggy memory to her, if even that, but I will always remember her generosity, kindness, and honesty. Thank you, Carly Simon, for proving to me that there is hope out there, and thank you for giving some of it to me.

AmyBeth Gardner

Obituary

I don't know you
but there you lay
in black and white
a paragraph
of your sixteen years

they forget about the time
your gum got caught in your hair
and you cut off
your only golden curls

or that time you flooded the laundry room
and missed your softball game
cleaning up the mess

but wait
that was me
and this is you

a tiny, printed section
on my page
next to an ad for America Online

"you can talk to anyone, anywhere"
but you can't
I can't
and that's what happened

had you planned it out?
like I had
what happened to you?
did you crash your mommy's car?
did you crack your porcelain smile?
did you get a C in science?
did you try to talk?
but were silenced
or worse
ignored?

you could have been like me
or me like you

sisters
in a cruel situation
fighters
in that high school hypocrisy

but I blinked
and never saw you in the halls
eyes never met
paths never crossed
life's little joke
on you
no more
than an ink stain
on my paper

Kathleen McCarney

3

FACING
CHALLENGES

*You'll make a lot of mistakes in your life. . . .
But if you learn from every mistake, you
really didn't make a mistake.*

Vince Lombardi

Still Handsome

It takes two to speak the truth—one to speak, and another to hear.

Henry David Thoreau

"I hate my hair so much!" I complained to my mother. It had bothered me all my life, especially in the winter when the wicked winter wind had a way of turning my hair into a giant knot. That day when I reached over and turned the heat on full blast, I noticed my little brother, Jason, was shivering uncontrollably. I figured it was from the chilly temperature, but it seemed odd that a half-hour later he was still complaining that his arm ached. Mom didn't seem fazed, but I realized he had been complaining a lot lately about his arm. The night before, I had awakened to hear him crying. I'd crept to his door and listened as he sobbed in the dark, murmuring about his arm. When I told my parents the next morning, they explained he was just having trouble adjusting to kindergarten.

The next day, Jay and I were playing in the driveway. We took out the new Power Wheels Jeep he had received for his birthday. When he rode over a bump and toppled out, he began to cry hysterically. As I scampered to him, he was screaming about his arm. The next thing I knew, he began to vomit. I scooped him up and ran inside the house. My mom and I immediately took him to the doctor, who sent us to the hospital. Jay cried the whole way; I had never seen him carry on like that.

At the hospital, we waited for the x-ray results. The doctor spoke to my mother alone and said Jay needed a bone specialist. We found that Jason had broken his arm and had bone-marrow cancer in that area. I tried not to cry, but I couldn't help it. I wondered why God would do this to my little brother.

If I told you how many times I went to the hospital, you wouldn't believe it. I told myself I had to be strong for Jay, that I couldn't let him see me upset. Our family had to be strong; we would get through this together. Once, when we were playing Nintendo in his room, I started to cry, and Jay did, too, because I was. He didn't understand what was going on. After that, I vowed I would not cry again. There was nothing to cry about; Jay would win.

I had no idea what chemotherapy would be like. I didn't know I would spend Christmas day holding my six-year-old brother's hand as he threw up uncontrollably. I never would have guessed he would lose so much weight, that dark circles would form around the sockets that used to hold shining blue eyes. Or that the medication swabs he wiped in his mouth would make him gag and vomit. This little boy went through much that many could not survive. He was so brave and so strong; it killed me to see other children running around while my brother was cooped up in a hospital room.

But, worst of all, he lost his hair. I recall sitting on the floor of his room playing Hungry Hungry Hippos. I lost miserably every time, which amused him. He'd toss his head back as he erupted in giggles, but when he shook his head, a clump of hair fell onto the red game board, and our laughter ceased. We stared at the wispy hair.

"Why is my hair falling out?" he asked innocently. I gulped and replied it was only happening to make him better. He began to scratch his head, and more fell out until the board was covered. I bit my lip so hard to keep from crying that it bled.

He looked up and smiled. "Do I still look handsome?"

"You look totally awesome," I choked out. "Just like Michael Jordan."

He started to giggle again. He took the hat my grandmother had bought and tossed it in the laundry bin. He said he was proud to look like Michael Jordan and didn't need his hat anymore.

That night, I cried myself to sleep. I was worried Jay wouldn't make it. This little boy who had not even finished kindergarten had to struggle through each day just to make it to the next. I cried remembering how full of energy he had been just months before. And I cried harder because it wasn't fair.

The doctor decided Jay needed surgery. We were so nervous, but he got through it perfectly. Finally, Jay was on the road to recovery. It was tough. It's hard even to describe what he dealt with. His hair eventually grew back, and he gained weight, too. One day, as I was helping him with his arm brace, I remembered months before when he was diagnosed with cancer. It had been winter, a season I despise because it was always so cold and windy, messing my hair into knots. And I remembered complaining how much I hated my hair. Since then, I have never complained again.

Julie White

His Last Smile

Because I have loved life, I shall have no sorrow to die.

Amelia Burr

The Saturday began like any other, eating breakfast and racing to cram into the car. It was Michael's last soccer game, and the parents were playing against the kids. As we neared the field, the familiar smell of grass and dirt wafted through the open window.

"Today's game is going to be the best of the season. I can feel it," my dad said as he parked the van. We all raced to unfold our lawn chairs. The heat soothed my chilled arms and legs. As the players arrived, a delivery truck rumbled down the hill and dropped off pizzas. The aroma made my stomach growl.

With determined expressions, the players and parents set out across the field. A sharp whistle began the game, and I settled in to watch. As the second half approached, the kids were ahead by three goals.

"Time out, time out," my dad called from across the

field. Dragging their aching feet, the players surrounded
the table and gobbled the food.

The setting sun drew shadows on the field, constantly
changing shape.

"Louloubell, can you scoot over?" my dad asked, and I
moved my bag to the ground. My dad dropped onto the
bench with a grunt. He quickly drained his water bottle.
Sweat rolled down his forehead and disappeared into little
drops on his T-shirt.

The whistle blew, and the game started again. The team
rushed to gain control of the ball and shot it. The sky
began to turn pink and orange. Just as the game was
growing competitive, I tensed as I heard my brother yell,
"Dad, are you okay?" and his muffled reply, "Yeah, I'm
fine." I felt my muscles relax and took a deep breath.

"Dad, Dad, what's wrong?"

I turned and saw my dad collapsed on the field, not
moving. *God help him. Help him. Save my daddy. I need Daddy
here with me.* I ran as fast as my ten-year-old legs would
take me to him. People were calling 911. Just as I caught a
glimpse of my dad's black-going-gray hair, I was pulled
away. Sobs overpowered me, and I thought, *My dad might
not live. I might not be able to tell my dad that I love him. I might
not be able to hear my dad's laughter fill the room, or see him swing
his golf club and send the ball flying.* Tears streamed down my
cheeks, and when the taste of blood filled my mouth, I
released my tongue from between my teeth.

"He's going to be okay, right?" I said between sobs,
looking expectantly at my mom.

She forced a smile and told me, "He's fine. He's going to
be just fine."

But he wasn't.

The wail of the fire trucks and ambulance pierced my
ears, and I cringed. The trucks left deep tire marks in the
grass. A crowd of parents had made a circle around him.

The paramedics pushed through. Minutes passed. I heard the anguished sobs of moms, which made me cry harder. The paramedics again pushed through the crowd, this time with my dad on a stretcher. They lifted him into the ambulance and drove away.

Later that day I was told that my dad couldn't be saved. That was it. He was gone. My mom was a widow.

Life without my dad has been like a peanut-butter-and-jelly sandwich without the jelly. Incomplete. But I will always remember my dad running across the field, sweat pouring down his face, and a contented smile lighting up his eyes.

Lyndsey Costello

Big Hollow Middle School
26051 W. Nippersink Rd.
Ingleside, IL 60041

Out of Love

It all starts with holding hands.

Winifred Aiden

I was five years old and loved my parents. I really did, with all my heart. Yet the atmosphere had not been the same for the past year and, smart little girl that I was, I could only partially ignore it, clinging to a bit of ignorance that diminished daily. The tension was always muffled at the sound of my footsteps, and smiles were always painted on quickly to present the glossy silhouette of a marriage to my eyes. But this time I was determined. I was so sure that I finally had a plan of how to fix everything. They were fighting in the living room about something when I strolled in.

I could feel it! My plan would fix everything once and for all.

"Dad! Come here, come here," I whispered, rushing him into another room.

"What are you doing, sweetie?" he replied, confused, as he gave in to my constant tugging. How I accomplished getting him to put on a dress shirt and that Italian suit is

beyond my comprehension. I assume it was the persis-
tence of such tearful eyes and the love of a father that kept
him moving along with the task.

"Stay here, Daddy," I commanded as I rushed into the
living room to prepare my mother.

I forced her into a shimmering gold evening gown, a
pair of stiletto heels, makeup, and a dab of French perfume
that my father had bought her before the descent into
phony laughter. She politely battled my pushing and
prodding; she, too, did it out of love. Everything was perfect so far. I was overcome by excitement, as if the head-
lines were soon to announce my victory over the
impending storm.

I pulled both my mother and father into the living room,
waiting to see their eyes passionately light up with love
and awe at seeing each other so beautifully dressed. I
looked and waited. They gave a faint, yet pitiful, smile to
each other and then looked at me. But neither smile was
genuine; it was the mutual assurance that this was all for
me, that there would be no actual effort on their part to
make this real. It was the smile that my premature wisdom told me meant they had given up long ago.

"Music, that's what I forgot. Wait here, don't go anywhere!" I shouted.

They stood there, uncomfortably looking at each other
with such remorse, knowing that their downfall had
affected me to the point that I would go to these great
lengths to overcome it.

My commands were no longer opposed. I made them
dance, and they did so willingly. I watched them waltz
with such a feeling of safety, with such an ecstatic glow
that everything was working, everything was finally right.

I could have watched them dance all night.

My bedtime came, and I pleaded for more time. That
night, along with a blissful five-year-old princess, the

royal ball and the joyful melodies were tucked away. The scent of French perfume lingered but a day and then disappeared forever.

Julia Gudish

Saving My Brother

Faith is to believe what you do not see; the reward of this faith is to see what you believe.

St. Augustine

"Oh, my gosh, find him!" a voice screamed hysterically. I squinted into the intensely blinding sunlight and frantically scanned the vast blue horizon. Beads of sweat formed on the ridge of my forehead. My heart took on the beat of a drum, painfully pounding harder, faster. My breath came quickly, increasing in speed as my anxiety rose. With every new pump of adrenaline, an overwhelming wave of nausea engulfed me. Foamy waves crashed along the shore, stealthily swirling and swallowing, grabbing like deceiving hands. Seagulls screeched and dipped toward me, warning, condemning. The rustling sea oats whispered accusations of blame.

Suddenly, I heard distant cries, muffled by the wind and crashing waves. The scenery spun wildly around and around as I feverishly searched the landscape in the direction of the small voice. In utter disbelief, I caught sight of a flaxen head bobbing between two gigantic waves. His tiny, frail arms splashed madly in desperation, fighting the sucking currents of the undertow. I shot across the scorching sand, stumbling over tanned bodies sprawled out across the shoreline, oblivious to sharp shells slicing the bottoms of my bare feet.

As I tore into the water, I realized in horror that the flaxen head had disappeared! My weakening knees caused my body to collapse, and I instinctively began to swim to the spot where I had last seen my drowning brother. Surging waves tossed me to and fro, forcing bitter saltwater down my throat. The intense glow of the noon sun created a reflection of flickering flames across the surface of the ocean, resembling the golden hair of my brother. To my left, I heard a faint gurgling noise, then a splash. I turned to see a tiny, pale hand emerge from the water, grasping the air in agony. In one swift movement, I dove toward my brother and grabbed hold of a frail, cold arm. I tugged at his body and led him to the surface of the water. He coughed and sputtered and instinctively began to cry. His warm body clung tightly to me as tears streamed down his sunburned cheeks. I struggled through the turbulent waves and staggered back to the safe sands of the shore. My brother laid his small white head on my shoulder as his shrill cries subsided to soft whimpering.

An overflowing surge of relief drained the energy from my body. I began to shake with the thought of what could have happened. As I stroked the golden strands of my small brother's hair, my eyes grew blurry with tears. As we sat in silence, we watched the warm orange glow of the setting sun together.

Holly Hester

I Was Twelve

A "No" uttered from the deepest conviction is better than a "Yes" merely uttered to please or worse to avoid trouble.

Mahatma Gandhi

All of my life, my father drank, so it was never anything out of the ordinary at my house. He would come home, have some beers, get a buzz, and go to bed. Some days, he would get carried away with the drinking and become rowdy. Those were the days that bothered me.

In school, we started studying alcohol abuse and the effects of drinking. At first, I didn't relate it to my father, but after a while I put two and two together. I began to realize that my father, my daddy, had a problem with this terrible substance.

My father's drinking was never talked about in our home. I think I was twelve when I finally asked my mother about his drinking. She, of course, said he did not have a problem, and life continued just peachy keen, but really it was not.

My father's drinking kept getting worse. I wouldn't ask

my friends to come over because I did not know what shape my father would be in. As I learned more about what alcohol actually did to a person, I began to be afraid of him when he drank. Sometimes he acted totally different when he was drunk. I was so embarrassed by him. I knew it was not normal for him to drink so much; my friends' dads did not drink like he did.

Finally, my father's drinking got really bad. He was getting drunk every day, and he didn't act like himself anymore. My mom and I started to talk about my father's problem because it was tearing our family apart. We tried to get him help, but he would not admit he had a problem.

After a rehab center and many Alcoholics Anonymous meetings, my father was not much better, so my mother made the hardest decision of her life. She told my father she wanted them to separate until he was better. This was definitely not easy for my family. My dad moved out, and my mom, my brother, and I lived alone, without our daddy.

It was the greatest challenge I have ever faced. I had to learn that it was not my father who was bad, but it was the alcohol. I had to learn to forgive him for causing us so much pain and realize that it was not his fault. I had begun to hate him, and I needed to learn to love him again. Eventually, I achieved all of these things, but I will never forget how much it hurt.

After three months of being separated, my father was a totally changed man. He had a new job, new clothes, new everything. He completely changed his lifestyle. Most important, he had been sober the entire time.

Since my father had changed and had been sober for three months, my parents got back together. I was learning to forgive him, too. After a while, we finally felt like a family again.

To this day, my father has not touched one drop of

alcohol. He has been sober now for years. He promised us that he would never drink again as long as he lives, and I believe him.

Just like my father, I will never drink. I know what alcohol did to my daddy and our family. I will never forget the challenge alcoholism gave me.

Tiffany Mitchell

The Best Haircut Ever

To fear love is to fear life, and those who fear life are already three parts dead.

Bertrand Russell

I am not old or wise by any means, but I've come to realize that we have experiences when we're young that we can only understand as we mature.

One afternoon, shortly before my eleventh birthday, I came home from school and threw myself onto the big leather couch in the family room to watch TV. Molly, my seven-year-old sister, was upstairs with my mom.

Mom shouted, "Jess, could you come up here?"

I groaned and tried to shift my attention from the TV to my mom's sweet but scratchy voice. "What, Mom?"

"I want you and Molly to do something for me," she said, her voice trailing down the stairs.

About a month before, my mom had told us she had to go to the hospital. She said she needed medicine because she was ill. I'd heard of people having cancer and knew that's what my grandmother had died of, but I didn't really understand what it was.

All I knew was what Mom said: she'd be well with time, but she would probably be weak for a while, and the medicine would make her lose her hair so she would need to wear a wig.

I ran upstairs and asked Mom if she wanted orange juice. She pulled herself out of bed, and this woman in her Old Navy sweatpants and baggy T-shirt (whose height I was rapidly approaching) told my sister and me to come with her to the bathroom. She looked at her thirty-something-year-old self in the mirror, her shoulder-length brown hair messy from being in bed, then gathered us in her arms and kissed the tops of our heads. I watched her get scissors from the vanity.

"Mom, what are you doing?"

"Who wants to cut my hair?" she asked.

"What? Cut your hair?" I was caught off guard. Why would any woman want her little girls to give her a haircut? The mom we knew went to glamorous salons and had the hairstyles from all the magazines she read.

I grabbed a lock of her silky, chestnut tresses and put the silver blades next to it. "Are you sure?" I asked.

"Jess, please, I need a haircut anyway," my mom pleaded.

And so I closed the shiny handles of the scissors and watched five inches of hair fall to the floor. Molly began to help, and by the time we had finished, my mother looked like she had lost a fight with a lawn mower, but we all laughed.

"Honey, I love it. You look like Tina Turner on tour," my dad chuckled.

"Mommy, can I cut your hair every day?" my first-grade sister asked.

My mom laughed at herself in the mirror. Molly and I laughed at our handiwork, and my father laughed at his beautiful wife with her new hairstyle. We laughed like we hadn't laughed in a long time, and the strangest thing was, we didn't really know why we were laughing so hard.

Every little girl loves to play with Barbies and cut their hair, put on makeup, and strut through the living room in high heels and pearls. Looking back on that spring afternoon in my mom's bathroom, I can now appreciate what an incredible mother I have. For a woman who was going through such a tough time, she helped her kids have fun, letting them cut her hair just like they would cut their Barbies' hair. Instead of having her head shaved in the hospital, she let her kids have fun with their mom. I am so lucky to have such an able, beautiful, and caring mother.

I thank God every day that she is healthy again, and I thank her for helping me be a better person, and giving me the best guidance I think any parent can give a child. Now that she is well, she goes to her stylist to get her hair cut, and always comes back looking like her glamorous and radiant self. Despite all the blow dryers, hairspray, and expensive scissors, though, she always reminds me that I gave her the best haircut she ever had.

Jessie Spellman

Apple Orchard

If you're afraid to die, you will not be able to live.

James Baldwin

We searched endlessly for a tree with apples that were just right: big enough (the size of a fist), sweet enough, but a bit sour, and flawless (no abrasions or rotted parts). My attention was drawn to trees with dark red apples clinging to the branches in great clusters. Our hopes of finding McIntoshes deteriorated. After biting into one, I found these were Red Delicious apples: yum. I began to gather these in my bag while Mother went off on her own search.

When my bag was half full, she reappeared holding out a McIntosh. I bit into it, exclaiming, "Where did you get it?"

She pointed to a tree near the swamp. My smile turned to a frown when I realized they were too high for my five-foot, two-inch body. There were apples scattered on the ground; I grabbed one of the rotted carcasses and hurled it into the tree. The apples fell all around me. Each time I tried to catch the falling sweetness, my hands would gather about my head.

One apple even got stuck up high in the vee of the branch. My mother began to laugh even harder. I hadn't noticed, but as her tone increased, I knew she had been laughing the whole time. In fact, we both laughed. I threw a few more up.

My mother helped me gather the harvest, saying, "These are enough."

She was afraid I might get hurt. *Hurt, how silly. I play field hockey,* I thought proudly. *I have hard objects hurling toward me all the time.* I even felt the scare of a bloody nose once from one of those field hockey sticks. A little apple couldn't hurt me.

Ouch, well not that much. I grabbed one final apple, enjoying the fruits of my labor, literally. We headed back through the grove, the overgrown, pressed-down, tangled grass, and I looked over my shoulder at the swamp. The water was green on the surface from algae. The trees were gray, with broken bark forming incomplete puzzles. It was flooded with light from the sun, yet the scene appeared full. I smiled at the landscape as the lackluster apples donated a tinge of red to the picture. The swamp's beauty remained with me even though it was not bright.

I turned, walking quickly with a hop just large enough to catch up to my already-departing mother. She pointed out trees containing possible on-the-run candidates. I gathered more Red Delicious for my father. I thought how happy he would be at our having thought of him. He was the one who really loved them. We began to walk up slight slants in the land to each new line of trees toward the store where we'd pay.

I had been noticing the grass with its strands faded green, weathered by the rain and frost. Once again, I had fallen behind my mother. Her pace was constant as opposed to curious stopping feet. As I approached her, I could hear a panting, wheezing sound.

I've always known she had a lung disease, but at that moment the reality thrust itself closer, hitting my consciousness like a bullet shot from a rifle. She had to stop, catching her breath, her chest heaving, gasping for air. The remainder of our walk passed step by step. Each pace passed, beating irregularly against the ground, in tune with her breathing, but without real rhythm. I thought of the altitude. *Step.* The cold air. *Step.* The day I found out she had the illness. *Pause.*

She was talking to my father. Something about "with my lungs the way they are." I became afraid. *Step.* Not knowing what it was all about. Some disease . . . no cure. *Step.* I did a report on it once as an excuse to look into the foreign words. It was so rare: sarcoidosis. *Step.* So little research had been done. *Step.*

She didn't want to take the drugs because of the side effects. "Mind over matter is all I need." She knew what would happen if she took the treatments again. In pictures, she looked obese. The steroids had made her body swell. *Step.* She didn't want to go through that again. *Pause.*

Her x-rays are illegible from the damage done by the disease. *Step.* She could even have lung cancer, and they wouldn't be able to tell. *Step.* The doctors wouldn't take a CAT scan of her lungs to see if there were anything else wrong besides the sarcoidosis. Too much money. *Step.* What is money compared to the life of a mother, wife, sister, friend?

She is dying. *Step.* The doctors are amazed that she's made it this far without steroids. She's fifty. How much longer will she stay here with me? *Step.* I thought that my only option was to make her final months, years, as pleasant as possible. No, that wouldn't do. *Step.*

What makes our mother-daughter relationship so close is our differences. Those little disagreements when each walks away a little wiser, a little bit more understanding.

We see eye-to-eye, singly in each conversation, and together as a whole. Love binds us. *Step.* I know she has little time left with me. She is dying, faster than she should. A little bit quicker each day. *Step.* Our apple groves make her immortal, though. I will always remember.

Natascha Batchelor

Exit: My Hero

For some, life lasts a short while, but the memories it holds last forever.

Laura Swenson

You could never tell from the outside of the building that there was an apartment inside, but of course Jay was always different. The smell of leather penetrated your nostrils as soon as you entered. Everything was out of the ordinary and extremely expensive, but that was him. He was not just my uncle; he was my friend; he was my hero; he was Jay.

A rush of memories have recently flooded my mind. I remember when I was five years old and a flower girl in his wedding and later wondered why he got a divorce. I remember looking out his bedroom window and watching the traffic below, hearing the cheering of the crowd at the baseball game, and eating at the Chinese restaurant near his apartment.

I remember when he took my sister and me on trips through the city to the top of the tallest buildings and the grand opening of that record store to shop. Jay was the most outrageous shopper. Every time we visited, he would say, "Did you see what I bought?" It was always something extravagant and very cool, but that was Jay. Now I know where I got my expensive taste.

As we grew older, though, the trips and sleepovers stopped. We would go for short visits, and a few times my grandmother and I would go and help him work in his garden.

Then things got worse. The garden became too much for him. In fact, the city got to be too much. Jay needed someone with him all the time, and it was easier for him to move back home. So he completely redid the upstairs of my grandmother's house. It was amazing! It looked exactly like his old apartment, only smaller. It even smelled of leather, and he still had something new every time I saw him.

Things were different now. My visits were reduced to sitting on his leather couch and watching TV, so Jay would have someone there with him while he dozed. It began to get very difficult, but I wanted to do anything possible. I knew he had limited time left, and I wanted to spend as many hours with him as I could.

I have clear memories of playing cards, happily making him something to eat, or taking him for short walks in his wheelchair. Still later, I would sit in a dark bedroom staring out the window while monitoring his intravenous tubes and thinking he didn't have much time left. I tried to prepare myself, but that didn't work.

On January 9, I had been looking forward to sleeping in. I was surprised to be woken up at 8:30 AM by my dad.

"Amanda, Jay died this morning, hon." I was in shock. AIDS had taken my hero away.

Jay lived longer than most AIDS patients, but that was not the only difference.

Jay had decided early that he would not let AIDS lick

him. He went to schools to teach kids the dangers of this disease, spoke at conferences, worked with the AIDS Action Committee, and, most of all, worked with our family.

Although it has been hard since he died, I have thought a lot about how Jay affected my life. He taught me about love, strength, and courage. If it weren't for him, I would not have been strong enough to make it through. He was and always will be my hero. No one in the world had more courage. I remember wondering how I could tell him, so I wrote Jay a poem thanking him for all he had done. It was his Christmas gift.

On Christmas Eve, my family went to my grandmother's house as usual. When Jay was alone, I went upstairs to see him. I gave him the poem wrapped in a box and watched him open it with difficulty because his fingers were swollen.

I watched him read the poem. When he was done, he looked up through his tears, saying, "This is the best present I've ever gotten!" He hugged me. Afterward, he told me it was very adult of me to tell him that it was okay to die. He had fought long and hard, and it was okay to let go. That hug is so vivid. It was the last time I saw him. I should be thankful I got to say good-bye and, most of all, tell him how I felt.

Some people feel that bad things happen to people because they deserve it, but no one deserves AIDS, especially Jay. Of course, he was not perfect. Sometimes, he was obnoxious and arrogant, but that was Jay, and he was special. He touched the hearts of everyone he met and made a little space there. When he died, his soul broke into a million pieces and went to all those little spaces. Yes, a light went out that Sunday morning, but it is still shining brightly in my heart.

Amanda Caryn O'Loughlin

[EDITORS' NOTE: *Here is an excerpt from Amanda's poem that was read at Jay's funeral.*]

> *You are always there*
> *You give me strength*
> *And for all of this*
> *I must give you thanks*
>
> *It should be*
> *The other way around*
> *I should be helping you*
> *When you are down*
>
> *So when the pain is too much to bear*
> *and I cannot be there*
> *Take this poem and read it through*
> *And know that I will always love you!*

One Tear for Bravery

Many waters cannot quench love; rivers cannot wash it away.

Song of Solomon 8:7

It's amazing how one phone call can make your whole world come apart. August 13, 2004, is a day I will never forget.

Away from home with my dad for the summer, I called my mom to check in, only to discover she was crying.

"Mom, what's wrong?" I asked.

"Put your dad on the phone," she commanded.

I handed the phone to my dad, and seconds later he froze.

"Oh, no," he said and handed the phone back to me. By that time, I knew something was really wrong. I begged my mother to tell me, and finally, she blurted, "Kane's been killed."

I turned ice cold and numb. I couldn't cry. I couldn't move. I couldn't even speak. If I'd been standing on hot coals, I wouldn't have felt them.

Three Marines had broken the news to my mom, and

two others met with our family a few days later to talk about funeral arrangements and benefits. No one cared about benefits; we just wanted my brother back. By the end of the day, these two had become part of the family. We began cracking jokes and relaxing a little, but under those laughs, we were full of tension and pain. One of them later told me that he would rather go back to Iraq and risk being killed than have to report to families whose loved ones had been killed or gone missing.

A member of my family has served in every war. My brother is the only one who hasn't made it home alive. That fateful day, he was returning from a mission in Al Anbar, Iraq. He was in a line of four Hummers, and his was the lightest. The first and heaviest Hummer passed over the mine. Nothing happened. The second Hummer passed, and still nothing. Then came my brother's. It was almost past the mine when it exploded, nicking his back tire. It knocked the driver unconscious, blew another soldier thirty feet out of the vehicle, and my brother, who was stuck in back, was thrown forward, hitting his head. He was the only one killed. The mileage on the Hummer was 666.

No media was allowed at the viewing, only our family and friends. I had not cried. I nervously walked through the front door of the funeral home and, in the distance, I could see part of his face above the edge of the casket. As I got closer, I noticed a neatly folded American flag covering the bottom half of the coffin. I felt my heart beginning to sink, but I kept going. As I got closer, I could hear my heartbeat growing louder and louder. It felt like it was going to jump out of my chest. Finally, I reached the coffin, took a look inside, and completely lost it. That second, I knew it was true. My brother was never coming back.

How could this be? My only brother, who had done nothing wrong, was dead at the age of twenty. I ran to the back of the room, shaking uncontrollably. I couldn't believe what I had seen. After my mom and cousin calmed me down, I went to look at him again. I knew I would never get another hug from him.

Time has passed, and it still hasn't completely sunk in. I'm still waiting for him to come home or to call. It bothers me when I hear people say there's nothing worth fighting for. My brother fought for our right to be free. And I will always be proud of him.

Ashley Johnston

Room 103

*N*othing *in life is to be feared. It is only to be understood.*

Marie Curie

Room 103. This number will forever be stuck in my memory. Sitting in Room 103, my mother faced the chance of never seeing her husband, friends, family, and children again.

Room 103 is where my mother was diagnosed with cancer. It's where she went through chemotherapy, lost her hair, underwent surgery, and survived. When I first went into Room 103 to see her, I didn't recognize her. Where was her creamy skin and thick chestnut hair? Instead, she was pale and wearing a sky-blue turban. It was almost as if she had been a butterfly, but turned back into a caterpillar. One thing remained, though—her smile.

It was the smile I've grown up with, the smile that made me feel better in second grade when I left my blanket at Grandma's house and thought the world would end. The smile that made me feel better at soccer practice in fourth grade when I fell in the mud and then wanted to crawl back in it with embarrassment. Many times, that smile made me want to try again, and not give up. Her smile was the sun on a cloudy day.

Sitting there in Room 103, why was she smiling? How could she be smiling? She was sitting there in the blinding white room with an evil nurse glaring at her from the front desk. She was looking at wigs in a catalog and eating Jell-O and creamed corn with tubes and needles stuck in her. There was a chance she would never make it out of Room 103 or that hospital. But still, she had a smile on her face.

Maybe it was the chemotherapy that saved her. Maybe it was the doctors and nurses who saved her. I think it was that smile. That courage and determination kept my mother going. It didn't matter that she lost all her hair or had to undergo painful treatment. Instead of looking at the darkness, she looked for the light.

So, whether you're in Room 103, on the basketball court, or trying to ace a math test, keep a smile, a positive attitude, and hope for the best. It can do wonders. It did for my mom.

Courtney Kersten

Honey. Sweetie. Darling.

Tell me about your problems, how
they're "personal." Sit me down in the
living room, on that faded red leather couch—
the one my baby self nearly ruined—and patronize me in
every way you can. Talk down to me—
"We still love you; nothing will change;
don't worry; you'll still see us both;
we don't hate each other; we're not in love anymore"—
and pretend like I'm believing you. Use words like
    "honey," "sweetie," "darling," and make this sound like
some joyous occasion. Ignore me when my breathing gets
heavy, reality sets in, and my eyes turn white.
Pat me on the back.
Call me "sport" for being so "understanding" of your
"personal" problems. Tell me about your divorce, how it
won't affect me at all. And I'll tell you how I knew
this was coming.

Jason Sherwood

4

LOVE STORIES

Love is the true means by which the world is enjoyed: our love to others and others' love to us.

Thomas Traberne

It Was Real

Courage conquers all things.

Ovid

It was real. The night was real. Everything happened, but unlike in a dream, it really happened. No one was dreaming. Dreams don't feel this real, and sometimes, even if you're not dreaming, your eyes are still shut. You want so much for your dreams to come true that you don't care about anything else. You don't care when or how or what you have to give up for that dream. This isn't about anybody's dream; it happened.

That day it had snowed, and snowed pretty hard, too. I spent the day at his house because that's the only place I wanted to be. My curfew was 10:00 PM, so that's when we left.

Stepping outside, we saw that his car was almost buried in a thick coat of snow, and he sighed at the thought of having to brush it off. I subtly suggested that we walk home, and he jumped at the idea, even though it was freezing. We began walking toward my house . . . snow falling down.

Walking home was just like the countless nights of years

past when he had walked me home—before he got his car, of course. He was my best friend in the world, and he still is. That's really important to me in a boyfriend—to be able to be friends, too—to know that even if he were a girl, we'd still be best friends. We talked about Christmas (since it was Christmas night) and the magic that it used to hold.

I told him how I remember being little and waking up on Christmas morning. There was a different feeling, as if that day was truly special. Christmas had magic, and the past few years it just hadn't. It feels like an ordinary day when gifts are exchanged. It's nice and all, but it just wasn't the same. We talked a lot about Christmas magic that night.

He walked me to my door where he stopped and smiled. His smile was big and excited, like he'd never been happier. It made me feel good all over. It felt like magic. We hugged good night, real sweet, and as I pulled away, I whispered, "Thank you . . . for putting the magic back in Christmas."

He smiled again, as I knew he would. He nodded and kissed me again. "Good night," he whispered. He stood, waiting until I got inside to turn away.

I looked around once more, at the snow falling down. It was beautiful. Then I said good night and went inside.

Sometimes I cry. I just break down and cry. I don't always have a reason; it just happens. I think I can blame it on the fact that I'm a girl. Girls do strange things like that, you know. Anyway, when I got inside that night, I just cried. I bawled my eyes out. I went to my room, and I sat on the floor and cried. This time it wasn't because I was sad. Instead, I was so happy, happier than I'd ever been or ever thought I could be. Things that made me unhappy didn't even matter anymore. I had fallen in love with him. I couldn't help it. *When had this happened? Why didn't I see it coming?*

It wasn't like before; my eyes weren't shut this time. They were wide open. He wasn't the perfect Prince Charming, and he had his flaws. But it seemed like the kind of flaws I looked for in a guy. I didn't want Prince Charming; that would be too much pressure on me. I didn't even want a guy who treated me like a princess, who would make me uncomfortable. I just wanted a guy who would be my best friend, and who better than my best friend? Everything felt perfect, and right.

I thought about books I'd read, newspaper articles, stories of people who never said that one special thing to the one they loved most. I didn't want to be one of those people. I didn't want to go another minute without saying it. *Okay*, I decided, *the very next time I see him, I'll tell him how I feel.*

I stood up, wiping my tears away, and looked out my window at the snow. There he was, walking under the streetlight, snow falling down. It was beautiful. I needed to tell him right now, so I put my coat back on and ran outside. I didn't even think about the curfew I was breaking. My mind was set; I knew exactly what I was doing, and nothing mattered. I didn't have a plan. All I knew and all I cared was that I loved him, and I had to tell him.

I ran until I could see him in the distance. Looking at him through the falling snow, I knew that he was just what I needed, all that I needed. I stopped for a minute to think about the risk I was taking. *He might not . . . in fact, he probably wouldn't, say those words back.* I knew he had never said them to any girl, so why me? *Why would he suddenly feel like saying them? But who cares? It didn't matter.* I knew he loved me anyway; I could tell from that goofy smile. It wasn't about him saying it; it was about me saying it. I had to.

I kept running. I realized I was still crying. The snow was still falling. As I got closer, he slowly turned around

. . . and I ran right into his arms and cried on his shoulder. That's the only place I wanted to be.

He stroked my hair and told me it would be okay, which is a nice thing to say to someone who's crying, but I already knew everything would be okay—better than okay. I pulled away and told him what happened.

"I got in my room," I sobbed, "and I just started crying. I cried, because . . . you just make me . . . so happy. I just . . . I love you, and you don't have to say anything. I just love you, and I need for you to know that."

He pulled me close. "I know," he whispered. "I love you." I remember all the snow in his hair and the melted snow dripping on his face. I remember the snow falling down.

I remember him picking me up, but he didn't have to because I was already flying. I remember the way the Christmas lights glittered off the snow. I remember when he kissed me, and his lips felt so warm in a world so cold. I remember when he hugged me, and we stayed holding each other a long time.

When he looked at me, I felt love.

But when he kissed me, I fell in love.

Snow falling down.

Stacy Boudreau

Nick

Tis better to have loved and lost than never to have loved at all.

Lord Alfred Tennyson

Nick is six feet, three inches tall, a handsome, muscular guy with brown hair, brown eyes, and a confidence-building comment always on the tip of his tongue. He's the type who would go up to an eighty-year-old woman and tell her she has great legs. He sweet-talks everyone.

We met at a conference and hit it off immediately. His charm was infectious, and soon I had Nick fever. We spent the entire two days together. When I arrived at dinner, I found him standing by my chair, waiting to pull it out. That same night, he took me onto the dance floor and taught me how to dance. The next day, he proposed and offered his favorite ring. We pretended to be married the whole day and walked everywhere arm in arm.

Nick was the first guy I could have really fallen in love with. Every time he walked in the room, I couldn't help but grin. It was insane, overpowering, and fun. After a great day, he walked me to my room and gave me the sweetest kiss on the cheek. The world was spinning, my heart started pounding, and nothing was more important than that moment. Then he asked if he could take me to my prom. He said he'd rent a white tux and a limousine and make dinner reservations. It sounded like my fantasy prom with a handsome prince.

The next day I was in a dream world, constantly thinking about him. I hadn't said yes to his invitation but had promised I would tell him the following week. I returned home still floating. I couldn't wait to tell my family about my new love interest and date for the prom.

Then it hit me. My bubble of love popped. Nick, my prince, was black. I knew my parents wouldn't approve, and my grandparents would have me dragged into the street and beaten me. I am an upper-middle-class, white girl from the suburbs whose grandfather once told her that the most disgusting thing in the world was interracial relationships. He added that never, under any circumstances, was I to date a black guy. These are the words of a man brought up in a segregated America, but they lingered. *I'm in love,* I thought. *What does it matter that he's black?*

Reality struck me right in the gut, screaming, *What will other people think?* What happens when you show up at a white, private-school prom with a handsome black guy at your side? How *will* you tell your grandparents? They would want to see lots of pictures. How would they feel to see photographs of their granddaughter smiling next to a black guy?

Not only did I start to question others' feelings, but my own, too. Was I feeling something I shouldn't? Was I doing something terrible? I decided that if I had doubts, it must not be true love. That's the excuse I used, repeating it every time I thought of Nick to make myself believe it. In my heart I knew it would be too hard to love him. I told him I had decided not to go to the prom and that I was really sorry. I think we both knew it was because of race. When I told him, my heart sank; I hung up and cried. I was angry and frustrated for allowing others, and even parts of myself, to influence me.

I went to the prom with a perfectly nice, well-raised, wealthy, white guy whom I forced myself to like for the purpose of justifying going. Nick and I have never gone back to the way we were at the conference. We smile and hug when we meet, but even then I wonder if my mother, standing across the room, is watching and questioning me.

I hate myself for allowing race to dictate our relationship. Race is a subtext in my life. I, like everyone else, tuck my racism away in the back of my heart where it keeps me in check. I've tried to suppress it. I've tried to ignore it. I've tried to purge myself of it by telling myself how wrong it is, but I am not immune to it. It may have stopped this princess from being with her prince, but it also taught me a valuable lesson. When you take the "race" out of "human race," you're left with humans.

Teresa Porter

"Actually, Kevin, Mom and Dad are kind of divided where you are concerned."

My First Kiss

The way to love anything is to realize that it might be lost.

G. K. Chesteron

Everyone remembers their first real kiss. The emotions, the place, and especially the person. Whoever said "a kiss is just a kiss" was definitely not referring to their first experience.

I had just turned ten when I met Deacon. He asked me to play kickball at our friend's house, and we decided on boys versus girls. When it was my turn, I kicked the ball, and it hit him in the face, giving him a bloody nose. After he got cleaned up, we played Truth or Dare. I was dared to kiss Deacon and was so scared I could hardly swallow. The big thing at the time was holding hands, and I hadn't even done that. Deacon took my hand, and I followed him behind the garage in the dark to share our first kiss. We stood there for at least ten minutes, both of us too scared to make the first move. Finally, he said, "It's going to be really fast. Don't even worry about it." I tried to believe him, but I was still nervous. He started to lean toward me, and I could feel his breath on the bridge of my nose. Just as he was about to lay his lips on mine, I sneezed, and the top of my head hit his mouth. Deacon's braces cut my head open. I felt tears running down my face that mixed with my blood as I fell to the ground. It was dark, and Deacon couldn't see anything. He told me I was a wimp for crying. Then I passed out.

When I awoke in the hospital, I had seven stitches, and Deacon was staring at me. I couldn't understand why he seemed too scared to speak. Finally, he told me he was sorry. Then he rubbed his head, signaling me to do the same. I saw my reflection in the monitor next to my bed and saw that my long hair had been shaved for the stitches. I couldn't help but cup my face with my hands and sob. Then I felt Deacon pull my hands away. I tried to resist; I never liked it when people saw me as weak. He had a good grip on my hands when he held them at my side, and then he leaned in and gave me my first real on-the-lips kiss. Deacon left the room as fast as he could, before I could say anything. I wiped my mouth and cried even more because he tasted like broccoli.

The next day, he gave me a card his mom had forced him to make that said, "I'm sorry for your hair, it's not that ugly. I used to have a bald spot once." After that, we became best friends. We did everything together, and two years later he became my first real boyfriend. After he would kiss me, he would always rub my head in the same spot where I'd had the stitches.

Three years later, Deacon was diagnosed with brain cancer. As the cancer spread, he forgot more and more. All of his memories of us were fading, and some days he couldn't even remember my name. I stayed with him through it all. It was a constant fight every day between me and the cancer. I would get so mad when he couldn't remember things. The cancer got so bad that he couldn't even leave the hospital.

One night, I got a phone call from his mom telling me to come as quickly as I could. I rushed to Deacon's room to find tubes all over his body that were helping him breathe and keeping his heart beating. He was only fifteen, but he looked fifty. I couldn't help but cry. I remembered when I had been the one in the hospital bed, but now my best friend was there. He held my hand, and everyone close to him was gathered around his bed. We all knew that these would be his last moments. By then, he didn't even remember why he rubbed my head, but he knew that it meant something to me, so he did it. He pulled me toward him and kissed me. He couldn't lift his arms, so he made me lift them for him to rub my head one last time.

He said a few words to everyone, and then he fell into a coma. When the doctors shut off the machines, everyone just stood there, as if waiting for a miracle. We stared at him for an hour before we could let go. Not one person in the room could stop crying. Even the doctor and two nurses felt his wonderful presence being taken away. Knowing that emptiness and memories would take his place filled me with sorrow. I will never forget Deacon, and there isn't a single day that I don't think of him. Who knew two lips could say and mean so much?

Katie Zbydniewski

Sweetness

Last summer we canned the peaches,
And trapped our memories in the glass jars
With the neatly labeled lids,
Sweet and soft,
Dripping in syrup and lazy summer heat.
We sat on the front porch of your house,
Looking up at the blue sky,
And back at your white house.
Our fingers were sticky and happy,
And it was then that we swore to be friends forever.
Amid the thick-blanket heat of summer
You reached over and left
A sticky trail across my cheek with your thumb,
Before our syrupy lips met in a sweet summer kiss.
I could taste the peaches on your skin
As you ran your fingers through my hair,
Leaving it a thick, tangled mass of
Interlacing words
Cut off by your gentle lips.
Maybe more than friends, you whispered in my ear,
And I smelt the peaches on your breath.

Now, long after our passion has faded along with the
   summer heat,
The peaches sit, neatly stacked, in a dusty pantry,
Their tidy labels starting to fade with age.
But I know that if I open one,
The peaches will be as fresh as our love once was,
And the memories will come flooding back,
As I taste the sweet summer scent of peaches,
Lying sticky on my tongue.

Emma Bodnar

The Hole in My Heart

Nothing takes the taste out of peanut butter quite like unrequited love.

Charlie Brown, Peanuts

He looks deep into my eyes, not with a look of love or caring, but of guilt. "Who was she?" I ask, trying to hold back my anger and hurt.

"Some girl . . . you wouldn't know her," he says calmly, as if not knowing her would lessen the blow. I try to look at him, but I find that all I can do is focus on the floor and hope the tears welling up in my eyes don't start pouring down. I can feel him slowly moving closer, and his hand rests on my shoulder to comfort me. I quickly shrug his hand away, not wanting the reassurance that everything will be okay.

Everything will not be okay. I want to scream at him and tell him how hurt I am. I want him to feel the pain I'm feeling. I want him to tell me he lied, that he never really cheated, that it was all a sick joke. I could forgive him for a joke, but not for this.

I can no longer hold in my emotions. Tears roll down my

face and burn my cheeks. I begin to sob and sniffle, and my head begins to hurt. I look up just long enough to see that he is also crying. *Good,* I think. *Cry. Feel pain. Hurt inside, just like me.*

We sit without talking for what seems like eternity, but is only a few minutes. We both are crying. "I'm sorry," he mumbles over and over. "I'm so sorry. I never meant to hurt you. I'm sorry. I'm sorry."

His apologies make me cry harder. I think of all the times he told me he loved me and how it all means nothing now. I think of him with another girl, laughing and having fun. He finally leaves me to drown in my emotions. I wonder, *Should I forgive him? Should I leave him? Will I be able to see him with another girl, especially the one causing all this pain? What should I do?*

I know no matter what I do, it will never be the same. There will always be an empty feeling, like a hole in my heart.

Olivia King

Eye Candy

There he is:
Book in hand, hair in face tousled perfectly
Reading a controversial book on philosophy
Fourth-period eye candy
I just stare
Concentrating on counting freckles rather than fractions
Sitting next to me
He reads contentedly
Eyes focused
He doesn't even blink as two jocks
Play football with a dusty eraser
Now the globe gets knocked over
And they switch to soccer
Soon pencils are rolling all over the floor from
The globe's "goal" between the desks
Everyone loves the chaos instead of the class
All the while he keeps reading
I dream my skin is the exact page he's reading
His eyes trace my every curve and feature,
    never missing a word
Just as I finish picturing his big blues
Rereading every inch of me,

The bell rings
He quietly places his bookmark between
Two undeserving pages
He leaves without a small glance
Left with only daydreams, I walk on
There he is:
Brush in hand
Headphones half on
Painting his masterpiece
Fifth-period eye candy

Stephanie Rose Xavier

The Master Lion Tamer

How do zoo workers do it? How can they saunter up to a hungry lion and toss it a piece of meat when they know they are in danger? How can they hand-feed a bear some nuts when they know it really wants raw flesh? And yet, the lion tamers always come away in one piece, untouched. That amazes me.

I sat at my desk, red with anticipation. The last day before winter break. Seventh grade. The day my friend had sworn to give his crush a present, probably the boldest act of his dull, boring life.

Jon. That was his name. Number one in Texas history, number one in French, number two in math, and next to nothing in the social department. His own personal lion? Jillian Klinger, who was, in Jon's opinion, the cutest, most beautiful girl in the country, if not the world. Jon had been dropping her little hints here and there: holding open doors for her, picking up her dropped folders, you know, the usual stuff a guy does. And all of it had been rudely pushed aside. But Jon, oh, he was persistent. Once, in a mock trial, the prosecutors had him hands down. Everybody knew Jon had chosen the wrong side, but no, his closing statement dazzled the jury.

And he came out victorious.

Anyway, it didn't matter if the crumbs were pushed aside. Today was what really mattered. Jon walked into the room as I twitched with eagerness in my seat. He entered the room with a big, juicy hunk of beef, lean enough that the lion would like it, with enough fat to please.

Chocolate. Layers of mouth-watering, dark, delicious chocolate. And encased within each confection was a nugget of creamy, irresistible peanut butter.

I shuddered in my seat. The lion wouldn't be able to resist.

Jon, the master lion tamer, walked into the room and surveyed it with the haughtiness of a chess player who knows he will win. He flashed a quick wink followed by a thumbs-up. "Today's the day!" he mouthed. He sat next to me, dropping heavy textbooks to the ground, and took out his special pencil.

"Wow," I remarked. "The special pencil. You're that excited?"

"Oh, yeah," he confirmed.

And then, the lion entered. She glided gracefully into the room, and Jon's excited face was exchanged for one of awe. Jillian walked toward her desk surrounded by friends, laughing softly. Her ponytail bobbed as she walked, and her face glowed. She was not thin, but not chubby, either. She was beautiful without trying to be. Indeed, she did not try to look exceptionally graceful, but her soft angles made that difficult. Her face beamed, her cheeks glowed, and her lips were set in a perfect smile.

For a moment, I almost fell for the angel myself, but I remembered my duty to my friend and pulled back from the brink. The moment she saw Jon, however, the smile left her face, a bird chased away by a gunshot. Jon had pursued her since sixth grade, and she didn't like that.

Good luck, Jon.

Jon whittled away the minutes, biding his time by

checking and rechecking his present. Was it beautiful? Was it nice? Would she like it? He sharpened and resharpened his special pencil, stacked and restacked his books, zipped and unzipped his backpack.

Finally, the hour arrived. Jon squeaked and stamped his feet in excitement, watching like a wary mouse as Jillian passed, ignoring his weak hello. When everyone had left the room, he burst from his seat.

"You know what to do," he said.

"Yes, sir," I cried.

I raced down the hall and practically fell down the steps after Jillian. I spotted her in the lunch line, pushing away a peanut-butter-and-jelly sandwich in favor of a ham-and-cheese.

I skidded around the corner, leapt up the stairs by threes, and burst into our room.

"She's good for another . . . twenty-five minutes!" I panted.

Jon flew to Jillian's desk, his face filled with glee. He placed the present on her desk and adjusted it. He walked out of the room, and then back in. He sat down at her desk and, pretending surprise, gasped at the present. A frown appeared on his face as he tried to discover which angle would be best to surprise her. He turned it this way, then that way, then back again. He frowned, then smiled, then frowned again. At long last, he looked satisfied and settled down to nibble his lunch. He smiled at our teacher when she came in. He smiled at his sandwich. He smiled at the board, and he smiled at me.

What weird things love can do.

Then, the rumbling came. The rumbling of a hundred seventh-graders returning from lunch. The rumbling of fifty seventh-graders racing up the stairs. The rumbling of twenty-five seventh-graders chattering all the way down the hall. And one of them was very special.

Jillian once again gracefully walked into the room and headed straight for her desk. Jon bit the handle of his lunch box to keep from screaming. What a nerd.

At once, I saw something wrong on Jillian's face. I threw a sidelong glance at Jon and shook my head ever so slightly. He leapt to his feet and buried himself in his grammar workbook. Too late. Jillian arrived at her desk and looked at the gift as if it were something she couldn't comprehend. One of her friends happened by her desk.

"Oh! I didn't know it was your birthday!"

"It isn't," Jillian replied.

It looked as if the big, juicy beef had something in it that the lion didn't like.

Jillian took the box in her hand and walked over to Jon, who busily scribbled in his workbook and tried a little too hard to look inconspicuous, his pencil scribbling too fast to be writing, his eyes too focused to be reading.

She gently set the gift on his desk and whispered something in his ear. He was shocked, and so was I. This was the gentlest letdown she had ever given him! I had expected her to rip open the box and dump the confections into Jon's lap.

As Jillian whispered, Jon's face grew pale, and then it turned a bit green. His lips parted ever so slightly into a frown, and then he stared at the present. She returned to her seat, followed by whimpers from Jon.

"Pull out your workbooks and finish page 562. You have ten minutes," we were instructed. Jon just sat in his seat, staring into space. His eyes seemed hollow, his mouth a thin, grim line. Twenty minutes later, when I thought the shock should have subsided, I asked what Jillian had said.

He turned slowly to me in horror and said in a low voice, "She's allergic to peanut butter."

Jeff Yao

"She's smart, pretty, and really together.
In other words, I'm way out of my league."

The First

I close my eyes and there we are
in a hotel parking lot
on the roof of your car
hoping it doesn't cave in
dancing slowly
even to the fast songs
you kissed me softly
you said you loved me
you brought tears to my eyes
sometimes you still do
and if I can't be the only one
to leave high-heel marks
on your car
on your heart
at least I know
I was the first

Dana Rusk

School Dance

One way to get the most out of life is to look upon it as an adventure.

William Feather

I had always been an adventurous kind of guy until I encountered the school dance. The dance itself was not a problem; my friends and I hung out, ate pizza, and listened to music. But then strange, unexpected things started happening. A few of the guys began pairing up with girls and dancing to slow songs. I sat wondering how it all worked. How do you know if a girl wants to dance with you? What do you say? Just then one of my friends came back with his head drooping.

"I got rejected!" he said quietly. "She turned me down flat."

I sighed. It made me sick to think that I could get rejected, too. How was I ever going to get up enough courage to ask a girl to dance?

In the weeks before the next dance, I started noticing girls in my classes. Some were too tall. Some were too quiet. Some were too loud. But there was one girl I kept thinking about. She seemed just right for me to ask to dance. The thought gave me butterflies. I knew I should ask her to dance at the next dance.

Fortunately, my friends encouraged me the day of the big dance, each with different advice.

One said, "We'll go with you and stand behind."

"It's no big deal," another said. But he had already danced with two girls. *It was easy for him,* I thought.

Then it was time. My hair had recently been cut and was gelled to perfection. I picked out my favorite shirt and jeans. I brushed my teeth with my two-in-one toothpaste with mouthwash and whitening ingredients. On the way, my dad gave me a pep talk. "Be confident! Look her in the eye, and be friendly." As he waved good-bye, he added, "Go get 'em, son!"

I rolled my eyes, thinking, *What does he know?*

Entering the building, I lost my courage. Walking around with my friends, I frantically looked for her. When I finally spotted her, I watched her like an eagle. As the minutes ticked by, my courage returned.

That night, her dark brown hair hung loose on her shoulders. The light shone on the glitter on her cheeks, and her lips glistened with lip gloss. Her pink shirt was stamped with the word "Abercrombie" and her bell-bottom jeans were hanging over white tennis shoes.

When the dance was almost over, the DJ announced that there would be one more slow song. As I began to walk toward her, I thought, *Should I really do this?* My feet grew heavier with each step. I could hear the music beginning in the background. The gym smelled like dust mixed with cologne. I saw her talking with her friends. When I finally reached her, I looked into her sparkling brown eyes.

"Will you dance with me?" I asked.

"Yes!" she exclaimed.

I placed my hands around her waist while she placed her arms around my neck. We began to sway back and forth to the music. As we danced, every now and then some friends would give me a wink, a nod, or a thumbs-up. *This isn't too bad,* I thought. *This is actually fun.* When the dance ended, my emotions were running wild as I waved good-bye.

On the drive home, I couldn't stop smiling. Not only had I conquered my fear, but dancing with the girl wasn't too bad either.

Adam Smith

Don Juan, Goldfish

The only way to have a friend is to be one.

Ralph Waldo Emerson

I don't hate many things, but yogurt and fish are two exceptions. I'm still not crazy about yogurt, but fish are a bit different. The story of one hero comes from the short yet inspiring life of my goldfish, Don Juan.

The summer before my sister left for college, her friend decided to buy me fish to keep me company. She invited me to go with her to the pet store to pick out the perfect fish. Naturally, I searched for the cheapest, most healthy-looking ones. We spent two dollars and left with five goldfish.

As we put them in their tank at home, we made bets about which fish would live the longest. We both selected a vibrant and lively orange goldfish. I identified a sickly white one as the fish who would die first. Boy, was I wrong.

I wasn't very good at taking care of fish. I didn't know when or how much to feed them, and changing their water was a chore. The first fish died a day after its arrival. Surprisingly, it was not the sickly white one. Day by day,

I lost the other fish until just the white one remained. I figured it would only be a matter of time before he hit the toilet as well.

Months passed, and the white fish was still alive. I grew quite fond of him, looking forward to when I would feed him or watch him swim in his bowl. I soon noticed, however, that he had some problems.

I would drop a few small flakes of food and watch as they rested on the water's surface. Don Juan swam to the surface and began to eat . . . the water. I watched this for some time and came to the conclusion that my beloved fish had some type of eye problem. The only flakes he could see were the biggest ones that only came in brand-new packages of fish food. I decided that Don Juan had inadvertently gone on a severe diet, some type of massive fast.

It finally hit me that I should go to the pet store and buy a new package of fish flakes to help my visually impaired friend. By rationing the large flakes and having Don Juan follow my finger across the water to smaller ones, his eating habits improved drastically.

When he was almost a year old, my fish and I experienced quite a traumatic adventure. Bringing him into the bathroom, I planned to transfer him back into his freshly cleaned bowl. Having performed this transfer many times, I had become an expert. I drained most of the dirty water until Don was left with just a little, then immediately shifted him into his humble abode. I hit him a bit too hard, propelling him into a nearby trash barrel.

Completely stunned and overcome with shock, I covered my flapping friend with a tissue, figuring he was close to death. I ran out of the bathroom, shaking. I returned his bowl to my room, thinking I would no longer need it.

My mother came home five minutes later. A frantic

mess, I told her the story. "Is he still in the trash?" she asked, heading toward the bathroom. I couldn't watch. I stayed far from the crime scene, praying my mother could revive Don.

I heard her shriek with excitement that he was still alive! I told her to put him in the bowl, forgetting I had put it back in my room. Using logical reasoning and quick action, my mother threw the fish into the toilet bowl. At this point, I ran to see my friend, but he had disappeared. How many places could a fish hide in a toilet?

With much luck, my mother located the missing fish and safely returned him to his bowl. I looked at his white body. Blood spots lined his fins and gills. He resembled the Polish flag more than Flipper. I figured he'd die, suffering from post-traumatic stress disorder. Once again, he proved me wrong.

This accident brought us closer together. I took extra-special care of Don and even planned to get him a larger tank with fun fish decorations for Christmas. Unfortunately, my plans were altered.

I awoke for school one winter morning. Turning on the light to get dressed, a black spot on my white rug caught my attention. Bending to investigate, I realized it was Don Juan.

Once again, I was a mess. I ran downstairs, screaming for my dad. He made the trek to my room and identified the body. "Oh yeah, he's cooked," Dad said. I heard the toilet flush.

I told all my friends the horrifying story as soon as I got to school. They laughed and expressed their condolences. I brushed it off, but midway through the day it hit me: my fish, my friend, was dead.

An autopsy was never conducted. Suicide cannot be ruled out; the place on the rug where Don landed was quite some distance from his bowl, which sits on the top shelf of a small bookcase. The fall alone may have killed him. No one knows exactly how long he flapped on the rug after suffering severe head trauma. My mom thinks the cat had some role in this mystery, but I can still picture Don's body in my head, and I am positive there were no claw marks. Also, the cat has never been very fond of seafood products.

My fish is a hero. He overcame adversity; it's not easy being a white goldfish. He overcame visual difficulties and an eating disorder. He survived one brush with death. I do miss him; I've never gotten that much enjoyment out of twenty-four cents before or since. His death was quite a shock, as was his life. Don Juan might not have done much for others, but he broadened my appreciation for one thing I had previously scorned. I'm still working on yogurt.

Lisa Kelly

Empty Love

There I was, being the complete opposite of myself, but for so long the pain was so intense and my tears were like a never-ending waterfall. Then things changed. I learned to cope, at least on the outside. But inside was different. I was lonely, hurt, and depressed. I was hiding it with a smile and letting it show with fits of insanity. When I met someone with similar interests, I clung to him out of loneliness.

I, the girl who speaks only her truest emotions, was speaking a lie. I was saying, "I love you," and in the process, making myself a hypocrite. It always upset me how people carelessly threw around the words "I love you," making them lose meaning. I knew I didn't mean it, but out of loneliness I tried to make myself believe that I did.

The whole time I was hiding the truth—that I was in love, but not with *him*. And against all my beliefs, I never told the one I really loved.

It was my good friend Jerry whom I loved so deeply. I don't know what was wrong with me, but I was so afraid that telling him would make me lose him. Two months passed, and I still felt alone. I was still saying those empty words "I love you" to others, hoping I could learn to love *him.* The thought never crossed my mind that Jerry felt the same way.

Then one night we were sharing poems and song lyrics we had written. He flipped through my poems and randomly selected one. It just happened to be one that was obviously about him. He asked to read it, and I objected so strongly that, being the kind of person he was, he wanted to read it even more. After twenty minutes of arguing and mauling my notebook, I gave up, thinking, *What do I have to lose?* Then he started reading, and my fears flooded over me. I left the room, unable to look at him. Later I came back, hoping I had worried for nothing. He asked me what it meant. I couldn't tell him how I felt, so I answered, "It's self-explanatory." But that wasn't enough for him.

He wanted to hear me say it. So, finally, I did. It was a bland choice of words, but it made him smile, hearing me say, "I have liked you since the moment I first sat and talked to you, and every time we've talked since, I have become more attracted to you." His response? Just a mild, "I think we can work things out."

I ended my relationship with the empty "I love you" and became myself again with Jerry. We would sit up late on the couch, Led Zeppelin playing on the stereo, while the whole house slept. But we would not let exhaustion win until the following day. Two souls let go on those nights to explore the depths of our minds. Nothing mattered but being close and lost in conversation. We have been together for three months now. I know it doesn't seem like much, but with him I've finally lost the loneliness, and for the first time experienced happiness. I know in my heart that we're in love and will always be together. I have never felt so wonderful, and the words "I love you" have more meaning than a thousand words. So with my whole heart and soul, I can now say, "I love you, Jerry."

Olivia Godbee

Six O'Clock Now

six o'clock now
we should be together
in some soft, quiet place
of maples unleafing onto the
blue blue sky.

six o'clock now
you should be parting the
hair off my face
with those eggshell thin fingertips,
occasionally laying a kiss along the
fixed joint of my skull.

six o'clock now
I should be watching you
in the pale grey light
a line of white in a landscape
of black shadow.

six o'clock now
you should be holding my hand
in a grove of sycamores unleafing

and we should be—
we should be
listening to the breath of golden
autumn fading into
the darkening wood.

Joyce Sun

"I got worried when she started to sign her text messages 'your friend, Janie.'"

Back to Life

The most beautiful things in the world cannot be seen or even touched; they must be felt with the heart.

Helen Keller

I never knew what life was until she came. My words pushed people away. My days were spent talking of life as if it were some dead thing that interested me in only the most abstract way. I was just a shell filled with what others said. A sheep they could lead anywhere they wanted.

I filled my head with lies. I could believe I wasn't lonely. I didn't need love. She saw through my lies. I resisted as her hands tried to pull me back into life. I was incapable of love. I would just hurt her. Her lips kept asking, but I couldn't understand. "No" was the only word I knew. She kept asking.

The first week I looked at myself. What did she see? My eyes were their same dull color. My hair went in as many different directions as it always had. I could still hear her words. Why did she love me? My heart jumped. I wanted to know. Her face lost all color as I said, "Yes."

As I sat in the back row with my arm around her (a move copied from some half-remembered movie), I could see what the couple on the screen saw in each other's eyes. I can still remember the moment when we said our good-byes. The soft glow from the porch light. The way our lips fumbled together. Her eyes as they sparkled while she gradually drifted away. I would sell my soul to live this moment again. Her soft giggle as her dad's voice called her in will always haunt me.

The world that greeted me the next day wasn't the same one I'd lived in for seventeen years. Something had changed as I danced home. The world was softer. Safer. She taught me to listen. I could feel what I had tried to ignore my whole life. For the first time, I could talk of myself. My mind started racing. If she could care so deeply for me, what about others? My family. My friends. I began to give back the love I felt. I caught myself smiling the other day. I'll probably try it again.

Before, I thought of love as some dead thing that could never affect me. My words would protect me. She helped topple my house of lies. I know what love is. I can understand what life is. She taught me more than any book ever could. I know who I am. I never knew what life was until I met her.

George Newton

A Turtle-Shaped Box

I had a dream the other day
That you'd driven me to madness
Obviously I couldn't tell it was a dream
I dreamt that, in frustration and despair,
I pulled the broken heart from my chest,
Half of it I sautéed with mushrooms,
Garnished with asparagus,
And partook of my own Last Supper.
The other half I UPS'ed to you,
Its former owner.
I admit
(You always know when I'm lying anyway),
A small piece I saved,
To appease the sniveling, sentimental moron
Inside me who still hopes you'll come back,
And I put that piece in a turtle-shaped box
On my chest of drawers.
This was symbolic
Some people used to believe that
The Earth was held up by a great turtle
You were my world . . . but not anymore.

I woke up with a strange feeling of pleasure
But I was just as miserable as when
I had brushed my teeth and gotten into bed
   the night before.
I wished my dream was real
You can't live without a heart,
It's very similar to trying to
Live without you.
I wish I was an ostrich so
I could bury my head in the ground.

Daniel Bailey

5

PERSONAL HURDLES

The task ahead of us is never so great as the power behind us.

Ralph Waldo Emerson

Weight of the Matter

I started out at 123-and-a-half pounds at five foot six. And that was a good weight. I was happy. I know now that I was thin, even underweight. And I wanted to stay at 123-and-a-half, five foot six.

So I decided to eat less.

I stopped eating breakfast. And then lunch. I wasn't hungry anyway, right?

My stomach would growl painfully. And it felt good.

Next I was weighed at 110–and-a-half pounds. And this was not good, the doctor said. My mother wept and moaned that she had failed. And I wanted to stop it.

Soon, it became a sick and twisted game. How little could I get away with eating in a day? How many days could I go without driving my mother to tears? How long before anyone noticed me diminishing to nothing?

Yes, I heard the stories. If you were too thin, your body would live off your muscles, eat away at your heart.

Heart attack.

Without calcium, your bones become weak. Without the right nutrition, you die.

You don't sleep.

No oxygen to your brain. You can't think straight.

You don't have any energy to do anything. There is only one main thought and action—lose weight.

And you are cold. Even in the dead of winter, you were never this cold. Layers of clothing can't keep the freezing out. Icy hands and feet. Numb fingers and toes. Blue nails. Chapped lips. Pale skin. Maps of thin, ugly veins.

In the dark, in your room at night, it's like already being buried in that box. It's dark and cold down here. And lonely.

And there's a screaming in your head. It is fear, and no one else can hear it. You don't want to gain weight. You don't want to die. You don't want to make other people unhappy. You don't want to be sad.

But you are afraid to be fat. You're afraid to die. And the screaming continues, piercing your eardrums.

Ninety-two pounds. A nutritionist, a physician, a therapist, and a weigh-in are your constant companions.

The all-important weigh-in that controls your entire life. 97. 104. 108. 108-and-three-quarters. 118. 114. 116. 119. 119-and-a-half.

Right now, I'm 118, five foot six, and FAT.

And there's no one down here to hear me scream.

Christina Courtemarche

Spilled Coffee

*You handle depression in much the same way
you handle a tiger.*

R. W. Shepherd

The dark hole of clinical depression is where it rains every day, coffee is always spilling, and someone is always dying. For me, it's been pouring for almost four years, and I'm stuck outside with no umbrella.

"I hate myself," I told the doctors. It had been raining six months before I asked for help. By then I was feeling hopeless and suicidal. This was the beginning of the pills, the therapist, and the end. There were so many medications and so many failed attempts to make me better. The green pills made me panicked and edgy; the blue ones put me to sleep for nineteen hours. But the white ones were the worst. I started cutting myself when I didn't think anything else would help; finally, I was sick of it all.

When people are sad, they cry, drag themselves around the house, and then call it quits after a day or two. A normal person gets the blues once in a while, usually over spilled coffee, a death in the family, or getting dumped.

The normal person gets sad; I get depressed. Sadness and depression are different. Placing them in the same category would be like eating chocolate-covered garlic. There is a point at which a person cannot cry anymore, when the point of no return is passed.

Still confused about the difference between sadness and depression? Imagine drowning at the bottom of a lake. It's oddly silent and cold. The lungs drag in bitter water that floods the lungs and stomach. On your muddy deathbed, a tiny red button is protruding out of the muck. This button has the power to give back your life as it was before deciding to go swimming at that lake. Press this button, and you get your life back. It seems the obvious choice would be to press the button. I would if I could.

The "normals" say it's all in my head. They tell me to be happy and to "smile, for the love of God." Well, at least they got half of it right—it is all in the head, in the brain to be exact. Serotonin and dopamine just stopped running around upstairs. The result is suicide or meds. In my situation, I nearly experienced both.

I woke up to a small Asian woman sticking a needle in my arm and taking blood. A larger woman watched to make sure I didn't get out of line. The strangest thing I can remember was that I couldn't feel the needle tunneling through my skin as she tried to find my vein, and I knew why. The night before I had taken 5,000 milligrams of painkillers. Though not enough to kill me, I was very sleepy and insensitive to pain.

I was in a hospital, a care center for teens with suicidal tendencies. I was told that I was in a safe place for my own protection. After the Asian lady put a cotton ball and bandage on my arm, I looked around. The walls and ceiling were white. A yellow desk and plastic red chair sat in the corner. The bed was small with a cold metal frame, an uncomfortable plastic mattress, and crisp white sheets.

The lone and tiny window had gray blinds and shed a haunting light that made me sick. I could see a sheet of plastic over the window bolted to the wall; it had to be an inch thick. It was a heartbreaking sight. "What am I gonna do?" I whispered. The Asian lady said that soon I would meet with my doctors.

After the nurses left, I went into my bathroom; it was so clean and cold that it scared me. The wall, floor, and ceiling all had the same cream ceramic tiles. My shower had a very high ceiling and a heavy curtain that made it dark inside. After stripping, I turned it on, but didn't hop in until I saw steam rolling through the bathroom. I let the hot water beat on the back of my neck and down my spine until I regained feeling in my toes and fingertips. Awake and no less inconsolable, I turned off the water and wrapped a towel around my gaunt body. I wiped the fog from the mirror and felt a lurch in my stomach as I realized that it was covered with the same inch-thick plastic as the window. Thinking about all the kids who had been here, horror overwhelmed me as I looked around the room—it was suicide-proof. There was absolutely nothing with which to hurt myself. The plastic had chips in it where others had tried to get to the mirror. Examining the wall, I saw chips in the ceramic. I knew how helpless they felt.

Gazing in the mirror, my body looked like a battlefield. Running my finger over the garnet gashes on my chest, arms, wrists, stomach, thighs, and calves, I winced at the memory of the box-cutter slicing across my skin, the line of red that followed, the beads of ruby that gathered, the stinging tears throughout. They were the cuts that showed the pain that stabbed at me from the inside. I believed it made the pain go away, even if for a short while. It was the only way I knew how to make myself feel better, and I hated myself for it.

I couldn't look in the mirror anymore. It was time to

cover up. I found clothes my mother had brought and found that I couldn't bear to think about my parents. Written in the bottom of the drawer, there were messages from people who had stayed here before me. The only one I remember is: "If you're not crazy when you get here, you'll be insane when you get out."

I spent seven days in that hospital, every day getting better. My life was given back to me, and it wasn't easy, but I now believe that life is better with me in it. There are still rough patches, but they're no comparison to the hole I was in before. It's been two years since I've thought about suicide. Everything feels all right now. Looking back, I can't believe how miserable I was.

The most important lesson I learned is to love myself. I may not have great grades or be good at sports or even please my parents all the time, but at least I'm happy with myself. Finally, I pressed the red button, and I don't believe I'd be here if I hadn't. Now, the spilled coffee doesn't even bother me.

Emilee Castillo

Where Is Perfect?

Accept everything about yourself. I mean everything. You are you, and that is the beginning and the end—no apologies, no regrets.

Clark Moustakas

It breaks my heart to look at her—her wispy blonde hair, shining blue eyes, and the graceful body of a dancer—as she stares at her plate and shoves her food around. She's only twelve, the same age I was when my life became a battle against food. She becomes aware of my stare and looks at me, blushes ever so slightly and forces a giggle, saying she's "just not really hungry" and had a really big lunch. I want to tell her that I know she barely eats anymore, that I've seen her beautiful body become emaciated from the pounds she has dropped, and her nails have turned the slightest hint of blue. I want to scream that, even though she's my little sister's best friend, she's like a sister to me, a sister who is killing her body. Only I can see it because I've been there.

As if it were yesterday, I can still see my mother's pained expression early in my seventh-grade year as she sat with me at the kitchen table, shaking her head while I cut my chicken into small pieces and shoved them around. I'd smile sheepishly and say, "Gee, Mom, this looks and smells really great, but I had such a big lunch at school," even though my stomach was churning.

No one was fooled, especially not my doctor with her crisp white uniform and tight ponytail who gently took my chin in her hand saying, "You have anorexia nervosa." My mother's face collapsed, and her shoulders began to shake. I hadn't meant to hurt her, or alienate my friends, or enrage my dad, or worry my teachers. I just wanted to be really good—no, perfect—at something, to feel like I was loved, worthwhile, and perfect.

When most kids that summer were out playing and enjoying life, I was surrounded by the dull colors and coldness of hospital rooms and IV tubes, followed by stiff chairs and interrogation from shrinks and nutritionists who, in my mind, just didn't understand.

My gaze moves from sweet Jenny dreading her food to her healthy, energetic younger sisters bouncing around our living room. I imagine them visiting her in the hospital, asking why she would do this, as she tries to explain that she just wanted to be perfect. I become nauseated as memories swim through my mind.

I sit with Jenny at the table and strike up a conversation about school and sports. She belittles everything about herself, from her grades and her appearance to the way her swimming times are getting worse. Compassion and sadness fill my heart as I tell her, "You can't be good at everything," and take her ice-cold hand in mine.

"I know," she replies, "but I just want to be really good at something, and I have no idea how to become that perfect." Her once-bright blue eyes begin to mist, and tears fall.

So, I do the only thing I know to do. I take her into my

arms, gaze directly into her eyes, and ask her the question that helped me recover, the question I would not have survived without. "Where is perfect? How can you or I ever know perfect?" Jenny casts her eyes down, letting her hair cover her face and whispers, "I don't know." Suddenly, I realize I'm crying, too. Crying unabashedly for the little girl dying in my arms. Crying because she doesn't know that she's already perfect. She is where perfect is. We are all where perfect is.

Allyson Klein

The Spigot

Life is like an onion; you peel it off one layer at a time, and sometimes you weep.

Carl Sandburg

She placed her slender, pale fingers around the handle, loosened its grip, and held a brown cup beneath it while the water flowed unevenly. The heat seemed to be engulfing her. The humidity, she finally concluded, was the reason she could hardly breathe.

"Stifling," she complained out loud. "Ridiculous." The girl blew her bangs off her forehead for a moment with her hot breath as the cup continued to fill with the rusty-tinted water. *Thank God I'm not drinking this*, she thought. She was young, seventeen maybe, tall, thin, and average-looking. She had a drawn-out look in her eyes, a look that told strangers she had been weathered, used even, older than she actually was. Peeling this layer off, her tan skin was evident, her long, dark-brown tresses pretty, even though she would never admit it. The girl waved her hands back and forth under the stream of water, as if it would help cool her entire body. She tried to smile, but the more she tried, the more tears filled her eyes.

"Hard," she said. "This is going to be hard."

Overhead, crows flew, squawking at the heat as she wiped the beaded sweat from her nose. She dreamed of the air conditioners in the store she had just visited, the department store with the television sets and the radios. Gravestones were all around. She thought of the families who must mourn the loss of those who lay beneath the glassy black marbled rocks. She marveled at some of the flowers and held the cup of water close to her chest. She had only brought one rose, one single rose that she had asked the florist to wrap with baby's-breath in cellophane. He had given her a peculiar look upon her request.

"But we just got in this wonderfully new pink and purple paper. Purple would complement this rose in a lovely manner." The florist had tried to convince her, but the girl again requested the cellophane.

"The rose will be outside," she tried to explain without being blunt, "out in the sun, in the rain, on the ground."

The florist was utterly confused, so the girl just smiled as he continued to place the ferns and baby's-breath around the rose.

The girl picked up her rose and the water, which now seemed even more ruddy. She walked slowly to the grave without a stone. There were no markers, only old, decaying flowers, and a few new ones with even fewer planted firmly into the ground. She had tried to visit this grave so many times but could not bring herself to do it, telling herself that the violent death of this person was hard enough, and she didn't want to be like everyone else, making a shrine out of where her friend was laid to rest.

Eventually, the girl felt guilty, and so she came. There she stood, breathing in the hot air and then expelling it, breathing hard, heavily, nervously, thinking maybe she should talk out loud, maybe she should water the flowers, leave the rose, and go. She looked longingly at her car. She wanted to jump in and drive off. She breathed in once more, placed the rose at the head of the grave, and kneeled, her hands clasped tightly, mouth chattering, face sweaty, and tears flowing down her face. She wiped them away, her body shaking.

"I miss you," she said in a voice that was trying so hard not to sound weak. "I miss you so much, and everyone thinks I'm crazy because I miss you so. They tell me to move on, but I just can't sometimes."

Now her words were pouring out like an overflowing stream. She found great comfort in once again confiding in her friend.

"They don't understand me," she cried harder, "and they tell me I have no right to be acting like this. I never used to cry so much . . . now look at me! The only person who ever understood me is gone . . . you were the only one."

She thought maybe now her friend felt guilty, so she gathered herself together and sat up tall. "You left me a lot of people to talk to—your sister, your friend Donna, your mother, the people you work with. But I'm just too busy comparing them all to you. I want to cry to you."

She didn't want to say any more. She was tired, exhausted from the tears, taking sporadic breaths. She felt relieved to have let out the negative energy, the anger, pain, and hurt. Finally, it was out. She didn't have to hide it anymore. She got up and brushed off her knees; they were imprinted with pebbles, grass, and leaves from kneeling. She thought maybe her eyes were red and her white shorts were dirty. She poured the water over the flowers, which they drank immediately—the geraniums, the pansies, and some exotic pink flower she had never seen before, with little blossoms and yellow centers.

The rose she left seemed insignificant. She felt like she owed her friend more but could find nothing else in the florist's shop that suited her taste more than a single rose. The girl kneeled, said a brief prayer she made up, and said good-bye to her teacher.

AmyBeth Gardner

Crashing Over the Edge

A few years ago, I sat at my desk. My hands grasped my head, tears flowing. One of many times. Tears of loss and confusion ran down my wrist, feeling as cold as metal. Why did I always think these things would never happen to me, never pierce my protective shell? To top it off, I did not have them—the ones I loved and needed. Jane, Nacie, and, most important, Becky. My friends. My mainstays. Tomorrow I would not wake at seven-thirty and leisurely hop into the car forty minutes later, happy, well-rested, and utterly content if only because I would see my friends ten minutes later.

Instead, I would rush out to catch a grumpy bus and dread the brief ride, an apple for breakfast. Then I would trudge down the rubber-coated steps of the decaying bus, entering this place of misery, masked in bright faces and cheery hellos. This place where concrete walls surrounded you and scraped you, with peeling paint flaking off, as if to remind you that nothing accomplished here was worthwhile enough to last. Where giggling twits in four-inch electric-green platforms flounced their primped hair, snapped their gum, and giggled. I would smirk inwardly at their pathetic behavior. But then my smugness would

be swallowed in the grievous truth that they had their
friends inches away, while mine were miles from here.
Then all that was left was to grit my teeth, close my eyes,
bite my lip, and walk past them to first period.

I hated it. I despised it. I was proud that I was not like
them. I was proud that I had higher expectations of the
people I hung out with. The expectations I had when I met
them. Especially Becky.

Becky was my best friend. She is a wonderful person,
but so complex that you have to love her to tolerate her.
She's like me. And she always tolerated me. Always.

And it was true. Through all my beautiful triumphs and
horrible slumps, she was there to whisper encouragement
in my ear and grasp me close like some Asian angel. Even
when I was a jerk, she stood by me. Even when I sobbed,
she stood by me. Even when I was cold toward her, she
stood by me. She held my hand and held me up. She was
a glimpse of heaven, but now I lived in an earthly replica
of hell. Maybe I made it that way myself. I honestly do not
know. But I do know that I hated it with such a passion
that I had to either kill someone or die.

I chose to die.

Each day I would cry many times, always alone, holed
up in a sickeningly barren room, cluttered with meaning-
less junk. And I would sob until my hands were puckered
with moisture. Sometimes my tears were not even shed
physically; I felt them sliding down my soul. I let no one
know. My mother had her own problems. My older
brother did not deal with emotions well. My younger
brother would not understand. My father was . . . I don't
know. Removed. My friends had always relied on me to be
strong, to know the answer to every problem with wonderful and perfect advice. They liked me superhuman.

So there I was. I was standing at the top of a waterfall,
grasping the breaking branch. I could not yet understand

how far I could plummet. But I knew that any minute I would become part of the icy water.

My grandparents' deaths cemented the deal. They flung an axe directly at the branch, chopped it so that I fell in. Fell into the rush that would throw me, freezing in its arms, over the formidable edge and crashing gladly into death.

I sat awake many nights, alone and totally terrified of myself. Sometimes I would throw open the window, feel the glorious gust of ice pushing through the metal screening, my cage. Snow was on its back. So what would happen if I ran outside to sleep in the darkness and blanketed in thousands of tiny ice crystals, covering my slowly freezing body? Would it be wonderful to taste my release? My mind flashed to Becky, sobbing and crying at my wake, looking desolate and blank. Then I would close the window.

One evening Becky was fiddling with my computer, searching through my files while I was in the bathroom. I came back to hear an "Annie?" Her voice sounded devastated, a little weak. There was a shimmer of something in my own mind, something hopeful. I looked at the screen.

My good-bye letter.

It all came out that night. I did not think, at the time, that it would change matters in any way.

But it did. Incredibly. Both Becky and I needed many "mental-health days" during the following months, but because of what she said to me that night, I could be myself again, be whole, be real. That night I had already plummeted far over the waterfall's lip, but it was Becky's arm that reached out and caught me. She stopped me. And now because of her loyalty and love, we climbed out and up the terrible rocks. We never slipped because there were two of us. And now, forever, there are two of us.

Annie Gaughen

A Forced Eruption

The worn, wooden cabinet doors slam open.
Shelves full of colored bags and boxes,
Screaming to me.
Chanting familiar songs,
I'm lured into their trap.
"No. Just shut the cabinet. You can do it this time."
Instead, my mind whirls in all different directions.
My red, bitten hands grab for anything they can reach.
Boxes are torn open, bags are ripped,
Exposing the poison.
I swallow, and swallow,
Not bothering to chew.
My throat is ripped and torn,
But I still manage to choke it down.
More boxes, more bags.
More cookies, more chips.
I look around.
A circle of trash surrounds me,
Like I'm some kind of enemy.
Trapped.
"Here we go again."
I drag myself into the dark bathroom.

The door shrieks.
It's warning me.
All alone.
Kneeling by the toilet,
It's something I now worship.
I toss my head back,
With a fist eagerly formed.
My knuckles already red and blistered,
From the previous gnawing of my teeth.
Fingers thrust down my throat,
Tickling my windpipe.
A human volcano erupts,
Spewing everywhere.
My throat is a raging fire.
Eyes tear.
Hair saturated with toilet water.
I fall onto the tiled floor,
Smashing my head.
With a flush,
It's all over.
With a bite,
It starts all over again.

Amie Barbone Powell

I Never Wanted to Hurt Them

Faith is the strength by which a shattered world shall emerge into the light.

Helen Keller

I am an oddball, a freak, a weirdo. I am loud and outspoken. I always speak the truth, unless it will hurt someone too much. I am popular, but not "popular." I want to dye the front two strands of my hair orange. I wear all black when my mom doesn't stop me from leaving the house dressed that way. I don't care what people think.

I also cut. No, I don't cut class. I don't cut corners, even though I'd like to. I cut myself. I use blades, knives, pins, my fingernails, pretty much anything that's sharp. Along with the bracelets on my wrist, I have scars. But see, the thing is, I don't want to die. That's something most people don't understand. When you tell someone that you take a blade to yourself, they get all upset and send you to counselors who put you on suicide watch, but I'm not suicidal.

The problem with counselors is that most of them only know what they've learned in books. Sure, my psychologist has a Ph.D. and a wall full of diplomas. It's a wonder she's still in her thirties with all the time she spent in school. I know she cares; psychologists don't go through all those classes if they don't want to hear about people's problems, and those who don't care usually end up in therapy themselves.

But my psychologist has never cut herself, and so she doesn't understand what I'm talking about. I try to explain, and I'm sure others have, too. She doesn't know how much better it makes me feel. Worst of all, she doesn't know the addiction I face.

I'm really not crazy. I don't need to be sent to a mental hospital, but I have trouble convincing people of that. Some express their pain in self-destructive ways. The kids who go out and get drunk to make themselves feel better don't get looked at the way I do. It is almost like it doesn't matter that other teenagers get high to forget their problems and it's okay for them to almost die every night. It almost seems as though it's overlooked that these kids drive drunk and deal drugs. The police don't catch them, their parents are oblivious, and so it's okay. So why am I the one in therapy?

Cutting is an exchange of pain. When someone gets cut, it's painful. Cuts burn. If someone is bleeding, she isn't very likely to be thinking about anything except the pain. So, regardless of whether or not a cut is self-inflicted, it distracts her from her other problems. All she worries about is the gash in her skin, and how much it hurts. She can't think about the fight with her parents, the bad grades, the falling-apart relationship. All she can think about is physical pain.

It's a great solution for people who don't like to cry a lot. It's even better for a girl who doesn't want to risk hurting other people to make herself feel better, right?

I used to think that. Slashing myself seemed like a good way to deal with my pain and not cause pain for others.

What I've never liked about people who drink and drive or deal drugs is that they hurt others, too, who shouldn't have to pay. It never seemed fair that someone who had nothing to do with a problem had to share its pain.

So, cutting was my outlet. It made me feel better; I could forget my problems, and even manage to smile. It worked for three years, until someone noticed my cuts. You'd think someone would have figured it out before she did.

And it didn't take long for what I'd tried to avoid to happen: hurting myself started hurting others, too. As people found out, it got worse. I hated seeing one friend look at me like he was going to burst into tears. Watching another struggle when she saw me was too much. They glanced at me from across the classroom, trying to make me smile. This time, it didn't work. I hadn't wanted this to happen. Other people were hurting for something they didn't do.

I don't have knives anymore. My nails are short, and my parents check my arms each morning. I caught both of them standing over one of the kitchen drawers the other day, and no one can tell me they weren't counting the kitchen knives and forks.

The furniture has sharp edges; so do pencils, and safety pins, and any other knife I can buy. But it's not for my parents that I want to stop. What makes me want to stop is the way my friends look at me. I can see how sad they are. The pain reflects in their eyes. They suffer because I suffer.

Addiction is bad. I know because I have one. I still can't see something sharp without wondering what kind of cut it would make. It takes every bit of will power not to try it out. Whenever I have a fight at home and am about to leave the house to get a knife, I remember their tears. My seemingly perfect solution has lost its sparkle. All I wanted was to ease my pain. I never wanted to cause pain for anyone else.

Lilly Aston

Six Minutes and Three Seconds

One isn't necessarily born with courage, but one is born with potential. Without courage, we can not practice any other virtue with consistency.

Maya Angelou

If you had told me last February that I would run a mile in six minutes and three seconds in May, I would have laughed. If you had then told me that I would feel robbed even with that time, I would have asked you to have your head checked. Then, of course, all facts pointed against such a reality.

I went out for the track team on a whim, a crazy, half-minded whim. Truly, my thought at the time was, *Well, running is pretty easy, and I need a sport to put on my college application.* Then I went to the preseason meeting. It came down to the painful choice between theater and track. My pasty skin and light-sensitive eyes seemed to single me out for the theater group, but I figured I needed a sport, and after much debate I decided to go for track.

The first day of practice, I thought I was going to die. All we did was the warm-up: two laps, a few drills, and a bit of stretching. After twenty minutes, we could go home. I had discovered all too painfully that my shoes were too small and that sitting on my duff at home all summer was one of the stupidest things I had ever done. I began to have serious doubts about my decision.

Well, I got new shoes and a little practice in before workouts started for real. Then serious practice began. Even though I'd thought it couldn't get much worse, it did. The first day we went for a two-mile run. I jogged at a turtle's pace for three-quarters of a mile and then was forced to walk. My breath came in jagged, painful wheezes. I was ready to quit. Unfortunately, casting for the school play had ended, so I was stuck. I kept going to practice, and soon my times improved. Miraculously, I was bumped to varsity halfway through the season. This is still a mystery to me, but I must have earned the position, which brings me to my story of the mile in six minutes and three seconds.

One Saturday, the track team was at an invitational, and the third race of the day was the girls' mile. Fifteen of us lined up on the curved white line, nervous energy coursing through our veins. Everything was uneventful until we rounded the corner on the second lap. You could hear our spikes crunching on the rubber field. Our legs, arms, and lungs were like clockwork. We were like a school of fish, with no clear leader, not touching anything, just flowing forward. We turned, ran, and breathed as one.

Then one of the little fishes tried to bound ahead and leave us all behind. In her eagerness, she elbowed me in the ribs, breaking my stride. Other eager fish leaped after her, cutting me off and tangling up in my legs. One girl decided to pass in the outside lane, breaking through my space when there was not enough room. My knees, hands, and elbows skidded along the track, gravel biting into my flesh. I lay there gasping for air and thinking only one thing: my status as one of the leaders had just been wiped, like me, along the surface of the track.

Runners flowed past me, some calling encouragement, but none stopped to help. Somehow, I stood, and although both knees, hands, and an elbow were throbbing, I focused on continuing. Then I saw red—the red of the jersey of my teammate at the front. The leaders and my teammate were 100 yards ahead, and I had to get to her. My breath came in rasps, but I concentrated on catching up. I made a dash on the outside of the pack. All I felt like doing was sitting on the track and crying from the pain shooting up my legs. Then, something snapped inside. That girl may or may not have tried to knock me down, but no one, no one, was going to take me out of the race that easily.

I clenched my teeth and focused on the leader. She was trying to break away but was struggling. There was no way, after all my work and practice, that she was going to get rid of me without a fight. Soon, we were rounding the corner on the start of the third lap. I was second and felt I was holding on strong. Then, with some hidden reserve, she shot ahead. There was no way I could keep up with her. I gave up. I knew I would regret it later, but at the moment I was just thinking about being second. That would be good enough, wouldn't it? Then another girl powered by. My adrenaline rush was gone, and I was content with third. But when another girl tried the same trick, I snapped.

After my triumph of getting up and going for it, I was not going to be completely defeated. A coach's words started screaming in my head, *Go with her, and let her take you with her! Don't give up!* I surged ahead with what little energy I had. Faced with a challenge, the girl fell back, and I sprinted to the finish line.

I had run one full mile in six minutes and three seconds,

a new personal record despite the fact that I had fallen in the middle of the race. I glanced down and saw blood dripping from my knees. My hands were bruised, my elbow bled freely, and my finger was throbbing because I had dislocated it. People kept telling me I had done a good job, claiming I would have been first if I hadn't fallen. So the joke's on me: I ran my fastest mile ever, and know I could have gone faster if gravity hadn't had the final say.

Emily Scavarda

Sassy

Chink. Clank. Chink.

That sound always reminds me of one day. I was eight years old, and it was a cold, dreary afternoon at the end of February. The dregs of a recent snowstorm were still on the ground, brown and slushy, and the sun, its light bright and cold, was playing hide-and-seek among the dark clouds.

The school bus had dropped me off at the corner, and I remember walking home, my cheeks red from the biting wind, and my thin legs straining to jump over puddles and avoid the cracks in the sidewalk. I had my special purple lunchbox in one hand, and in the other I clutched some crayon drawings of my family I had proudly made in school. As I approached my house, I broke into a joyful skip and frolicked up the front stairs and through the door. In the hall I shed my purple coat and matching boots, and, leaving them carelessly on the floor in a wet bundle, I ran through the foyer and into the kitchen.

There, the sunshine was filtering down through the many windows, with the square patterns of light playing tag on the wooden table where my mother sat. Oddly, she was in shadow: the sunbeams danced around her but not near her, as if something kept them away. My mother's fingers were wrapped tightly around a half-empty coffee mug. I recall those hands with strange clarity: the skin stretched thin and drawn into a straight line. Her eyes, usually merry, looked glassy and swollen, and I saw the tracks of many dried tears on her smooth cheeks.

Sensing that something was wrong, I forgot about the drawings I clutched and stood in the doorway, looking at her with apprehension. She attempted a smile, failed, and then pushed back her chair and rose. She crossed the room and squatted down in front of me and, looking straight into my eyes, began to speak in a low, gentle voice.

Thinking back on it now, her words escape me.

All I recall is thinking, *No . . . this isn't true—Sassy CAN'T be dead!* I ran from the room, ran from my mother and the words she had spoken, ran from the death I saw dancing with the sunbeams in the bright kitchen. I raced up the front staircase and down the hall to my bedroom where I grabbed my favorite Slinky. Filled with sudden urgency, I raced down the hall, almost tripping over Sassy's favorite toy mouse, and stopped, breathless when I reached the top of the stairs. There I sat, pulled my knees to my chest, and wrapped my thin arms around me, a small voice inside my head repeating, "She's alive. She's alive. She's alive." I sat up straight and reached for my Slinky, the familiar feel of its cool wire coils calming me, for I knew Sassy would come. I set the Slinky up against the top of the step and gently pushed it, my hand quivering, and watched as it began its downward descent.

Chink. Clank. Chink.

I kept my eyes riveted to the silvery metal blur, waiting for Sassy to come scampering to catch it as she had done unfailingly thousands of times over the years. No matter where she was, Sassy always heard that distinctive sound and came running, determined to catch the toy before it reached the bottom.

Chink. Clank. Chink. I looked over my shoulder and down the hall. Empty. "She'll come," I whispered.

Chink. Clank. Chink. I peered down the stairs to the front foyer. Empty. *She'll come,* I thought.

Chink. Clank. Chi . . .

The Slinky stopped, its silvery music interrupted by the bottom of the staircase. It sat still. For a moment nothing stirred, and then, in the too-loud silence that followed, I began to weep, for Sassy had not come.

Amy Hochsprung Lawton

Empty

"What did you eat for breakfast?"

I thought for a moment, then answered defiantly, "Blueberry muffins."

"Shut up," Jan* replied. "I know that's a lie. Now, go get some lunch."

"All right, Mother," I retorted, ignoring her command. I stared at her. She stared back. Why was she making such a big deal? The fact was I had eaten two miniature blueberry muffins. And if that wasn't enough to make my stomach hang over the waist of my jeans, what Jan wanted me to eat would. I tuned out my friend for the time being. Besides, maybe I just wasn't hungry.

"Hey, so did you read my note yet, Ashley?" I asked, trying desperately to change the subject. She saw right through me, becoming Jan's ally.

"Food. Go stand in that lunch line and get some food, and then I will think about reading your note." I was starting to get annoyed. Ashley and Jan were the only ones who knew, and they were acting as though I were a small child. I had thought that in letting them in on my secret,

---

* Names have been changed to protect privacy.

they would support me. They hadn't. But I didn't want anyone else to find out, so I said, "Fine." I got up huffily and made my way to the lunch line. When the lady asked what I wanted, I hesitated. *Nothing!* I wanted to scream. *I don't want anything. It's my friends who want the food.* I took a deep breath. "The steak and cheese sub, please." The sandwich looked lonely in the middle of that tray, so I added a bottle of water. The two sides of my brain fought.

Don't eat that, the first one warned. *You're already fat and disgusting; you don't need any more calories.* The second argued, *Eat the sub, and the cookies, and the vegetables.* The rebuttal came, *Don't get fat . . . don't get fat . . . don't get fat.* I tried to block out those conflicting voices, but they grew louder and louder.

As I punched in my lunch number, the lady at the register eyed my tray. Then she looked up at me and asked, "Is that all you're getting?"

"Uh, yeah. I ate a big breakfast." She looked skeptical. Not wanting more advice, I quickly snatched my tray and started for the lunch table. As I walked away, she mumbled under her breath, "No wonder girls are so skinny these days." Puh-leeease.

Making my way through the cafeteria, I passed a table of guys. All their trays were filled with pizza and fries and cookies. One saw me as I walked by and put his hand on my waist.

"Look, guys," he said with a laugh. "I can fit one hand around Lori's whole waist!" Damn. Damn their mockery. I turned to the trash can and threw the tray in it. Tears filled my eyes as I hurried out of the cafeteria. Opening the bathroom door, I looked under the stalls to make sure no one was there. Then I locked the door, leaned over a toilet, and shoved two fingers down my throat. I gagged, but nothing came up. I tried again. Nothing. I wanted to scream. I choked on my tears as I unlocked the door and, standing sideways in front of the mirror, flipped the tag out of the back of my new jeans. Size 1/2. It wasn't enough. I had tried the size 0's, but they wouldn't fit. Because I was fat.

Didn't anyone see? Didn't they see how fat I was? No, they always told me, "You're so skinny, Lori. You're so thin." I knew they were just trying to be good friends. I wiped my tears and opened the door to go back to the cafeteria, but I stopped. *No,* I thought. *You're not getting away that easily.* I returned to the stall, locked the door once more, and went back to work on the blueberry muffins.

V. L. Laurense Zinger

A Beard

I wish I could grow a beard. What does a guy have to do to grow some facial hair around here?

I'm a manly mountain man of seventeen years. I've done everything in my childhood to prepare me to be the manliest of men. I'm rough and tough, but for some unknown reason I can't grow much more than a patchy mess on my neck. And that's lousy.

It's caused many problems for me over the years. You see, if I could actually grow a beard, I wouldn't shave, and I hate shaving. But since if I don't shave for about two days my neck becomes a briar patch of grossness, I'm forced to shave daily.

And I'm pretty lazy.

I'm afraid that I just have a bad gene for growing facial hair. My dad has never been much of a man for growing a beard or a mustache. Neither has my mom. So I guess that could be the problem. I could have it worse, though. My mother's father had a nice full mustache in his prime, back when he was an aspiring sports reporter for the *Detroit Free Press*, but he has never had a single hair on his legs. That is weird.

My brother, who is two years older than me, faced my

same problem. He has always wanted to be able to tickle a pretty lady's nose while kissing her but has been unsuccessful. He grew a mustache once, but it was thin and gross. He documented it, and the pictures are family keepsakes.

Another problem presented by my lack of facial hair is that I'm playing a character in a school play who has a beard. The show is double cast, so I have a counterpart who will be playing my role for half the run. Even though he is a year younger, he has a full beard! I will be forced to wear a fake beard during the show, and not only will this be an insult to my manhood, I will also probably be too lazy to shave the days before the show so that when I remove the beard, it will painfully rip out what few hairs decorate my face.

Over the years, I've noticed that most girls don't seem to like facial hair. So why do I want it? To me, it is a sign of a true man. No one ever wants to mess with a guy with a beard. If you pick a fight with him, you are just plain stupid. Case in point: the fellow actor with the facial hair I mentioned is a black belt. Don't be dumb. Just leave bearded people alone.

It could be worse, though. I could be hairless all over. Also, even though I think my family has a bad facial hair gene, we have good hair in general. My dad's hair rocks. He is forty-six and doesn't have a single gray hair, so hopefully I won't go bald or gray early.

I guess I can wait to grow some facial hair. Maybe I'll just shave several times a day because I heard that helps, and I want to have a beard for the prom, even though I don't think my date will let that fly. And, when I graduate, I think I'll spend the summer growing a beard, so I can look impressive when I meet everyone at college.

If that doesn't work, I'm pretty good with a marker. I could probably draw on a pretty convincing 'stache.

Steven Jones

6

FAMILY STUFF

Call it a clan, call it a network, call it a tribe, call it a family. Whatever you call it, whoever you are, you need one.

Jane Howard

Car Talk

The average parent will go through the full gamut of ups and downs and trials and tribulations. The key is developing close times with your children, teaching them to perform and function effectively.

Earl Woods

I've been the proud owner of a driving permit, a small plastic card verifying my right to drive with a consenting licensed driver, for the past year. I am also, unfortunately, a very poor driver. Thanks to my abilities, the rear end of our small car has seen pine trees, poles, and snow banks, all up close and personal. It's embarrassing, actually. I am supposedly a bright, well-rounded student who should be able to sail through this one teenage rite of passage with no problem. Alas . . . I cannot.

The problem all started a year ago when that now-aging permit first found its way into my eager hands. Mom and I took our first trip around an empty parking lot. I was totally unaware that my mother was most definitely not the best teacher for me. It wasn't that she yelled or told me

I was doing poorly. No, my mother told me I was doing quite well but did so while digging her nails into the seat and trying to brake for me. As you can imagine, my mother's "helpful instructions" only managed to make me more nervous. A quick evening run to the drugstore, where I nearly plowed over a small parked car, brought an end to any hopes of learning from Mom.

Since it was obvious that I would no longer be practicing with her, the job was placed in the hands of my father. The idea of learning from Dad was not one that thrilled me. I love him dearly, but I just did not see Dad as someone I could be comfortable learning from. He almost never yelled, which was an advantage. But Dad also almost never talked. We shared a typical father-daughter relationship. He'd ask how school was, and I'd say it was fine. Unfortunately, that was the extent of most of our conversations. The prospect of spending hours alone with someone who might as well have been a stranger really scared me.

As we got into the car that first time, I was not surprised at what happened. Dad and I drove around, saying almost nothing, aside from a few turning instructions. As my lessons wore on, however, things began to change. Dad would turn up the radio, so I could fully experience, and thus appreciate, his favorite Rolling Stones music. He actually began to talk. It was a bit scarier than silence, at first. I was soon hearing about past failed dates, "basic bod" gym class, and other stories of his past, including some of his first encounters with my mom.

Dad's sudden chattiness was shocking until I thought of why he was telling me so much. In the car, I was a captive audience. To learn to drive, it was a requirement that I sit and listen to his every word. In all the years that I had wondered why my father never spoke that much, I had never stopped to consider the possibility that it was because I had never bothered to listen. Homework, friends, and even TV had all called me from him, and I never thought my quiet father had anything to say.

Since I began driving with him, my dexterity on the road has greatly increased. More importantly, though, my knowledge of who my father is has also increased. Just living with him wasn't enough—it took driving with him for me to get to know someone who was once a mystery.

Nicole Docteur

"This is Dad. I thought I told you not to answer the cell phone while you were driving."

A Familiar Stranger

A mother never realizes that her children are no longer children.

James Agee

My mom and I have absolutely nothing in common. Nothing. People always say that becoming like your parents is inevitable, but I am positive this will never happen to me. We are total opposites, and for the past few years most conversations have ended with me screaming "I hate you!" and then locking myself in my room.

It's not like we don't love each other—I mean, obviously we do, and I know that—but she doesn't understand me at all. She doesn't seem to understand why I'm not still afraid of boys, or why I don't tell her everything, or why I wouldn't want to wear sweat pants and a huge T-shirt to school.

"I know exactly how you feel" is one of the lines she uses to try to calm me down, since I usually dramatize situations. This always succeeds in making me even angrier. *You don't know how I feel! You have no idea how I feel!* my mind screams.

As I get older, I have thought a lot about my relationship with my mother. It's strange—she's the person whose face I saw first when I was born, someone I have lived with my whole life. You would think I would know her better than anyone, but I started to realize that I don't know her at all. Of course, I know her as my mom, the mother who made me lunches and sat me on the bathroom counter to clean my bloody knee when I fell off my bike, the mother I swear at in my head sometimes and vow never to be like, the mother I love. But I don't know her as a person. Sure, I've heard of her childhood adventures and some of her experiences in college, but overall I probably know my friends better than I know my own mother. This realization has given me a heavy, indescribable sadness. I feel like I should know her better . . . and I want to . . . but how?

I have looked through her dog-eared yearbooks, running my hands over the pages and hoping to gain some knowledge the pictures can't reveal. I recognize that expression in her dark brown eyes; it's the same one that stares back at me when I look in the mirror. I have always thought that eyes tell a lot about a person, but despite the fact that hers look just like mine, they say nothing about who she was. Next to her name is the picture of a young, vibrant, amazingly beautiful girl. Her shiny brown hair is perfectly straight, flipped at the ends and falling right below her shoulders. Prom queen. Captain of the cheerleading team. Valedictorian. National Honor Society member. Her many titles are listed below her picture, along with her aspiration to become a doctor (which she did). She was only a few years older than I am now, but I can't seem to match these labels with my view of her.

This young girl in a long white dress, smiling as a crown is placed on her head—how could she be the same woman who would live in her pajamas if she could? I scan the black-and-white group shots for her face. There she is again, holding up her pom-poms and wearing a pleated skirt and a sweater, her charismatic smile setting her apart from a sea of unfamiliar black-and-white faces.

But she remains simply a familiar stranger. What was she like then? Would I have been friends with her? What is she really like . . . not from a daughter's perspective? I don't know. And maybe I'm wrong about us being so different. Maybe we're a lot more alike than I realize. And maybe that wouldn't be a bad thing at all. I really don't know . . . and I really don't know her either.

Jamie Sarfeh

Leaving Dad

I used to think my parents were like machines
And programmed themselves with series of if/then
    statements.
If the child sneaks out at night, then deliver lecture #458.
If her friends are bad for her, then it's lecture #342B.

And they had concrete problems, not like mine,
which required crying over always
Because I am not a machine.
My life would never be perfect.
If the child is afraid, comfort her.

Then one day I learned that Dad picked up all the
    pennies he saw
and threw them onto playgrounds so the little kids could
    find them
and he knew that made them very happy.
That's why he did it.
Dad is like that sometimes.
And he and Mom sometimes stared at children running
    around in malls.
If the children are happy, then you will be, also.

And Dad watched me like that, too.
We'd be at a track meet, and I would be high-jumping
and when he was truly afraid, I would miss that last
    attempt at 4'10"
he stopped videotaping and watched
as if I were his life and responsibility.
If the child misses, tell her how to clear it.

And then I thought about how Dad would feel if I missed.
He would tell me that I tried very hard, even though,
    he noticed, I didn't lift up my knee enough.
Never, "I wanted to see you at State another year."
    Or "I wish you would have made it."
Dad rarely spoke of himself when it was really important.
Unless, of course, it was to tell a story I would benefit from.
If the child looks back, then smile.

But in the eyes of my parents, I can see them.
And how everything I do affects them, just a little . . .
Their computer responses are forced and hard
but beneath I decided lay something more.

Themselves.

And when I leave I will leave Dad behind.
He will help me unpack to go away to college and
probably talk with the other parents.
Because that's what Dad does.
And who am I to know how he really feels?
After all these years, he was always my dad.
Talking to me. Watching my fascinating life.
If the child must go away, then leave her to go.
It all seems so simple now.
They will let me go because that is their
    parent-computer response.

And I will say good-bye to them.
But I am older now and wiser
and want more than anything
for them to realize how much more
I know there is.

Kimberly Burton

Maybe Tomorrow

Past experience indicated that the best way of dealing with her is total attention and love.

Lyndon Johnson

I hate hospitals; they are cold and uninviting. My father is sitting next to me, carrying on a conversation with my mother that I cannot follow. I look back to my book. My mom is playing with a spoon left from her dinner. She smiles as she talks, but it's not really her. She is weak and vulnerable sitting there in front of me. I try to smile, but I do not recognize her. She looks the same, but here she is no longer that strong and fearless woman. On our way to her room, we bought her a stuffed brown dog that she now clutches playfully. I force a grin.

I don't know how I should feel. I don't really like to deal with illness or death. It's something that should never affect me. I know she will be all right, but I hate the fact that she is sick. I hate her for being sick, but I don't *really* hate her. I love her. I push the negative thoughts to the back of my mind. My mother starts to talk to me. Taking this opportunity, my father leaves. I sit uncomfortably alone with her. She smiles, as though she is signaling me to say something.

I try not to notice. I don't know what to say. There is a barrier of stubbornness and strength between us. She didn't tell me she was sick; she was trying to protect me. I didn't tell her I was worried; I didn't want to scare her. She'll be all right.

Outside in the hall, the nurses are talking about the elections. "You won't be able to vote tomorrow," I say. She nods. The conversation ends. I try desperately to think of something good to say. There are a thousand things I *should* say, that I want to say, but for some reason I don't know how.

I hate seeing her sick. She tells me to be good, to drive safely, to make her Jell-O, and take care of Daddy. I nod. Silence. I mention briefly my school day, the quiz I took, and what I had for lunch—things that aren't really relevant to this present situation. I want to tell her I love her, that she is the world to me, that I am sorry for the fights we've had, but the words are trapped behind our barrier. My father comes in; it is eight o'clock, visiting hours are over.

She smiles. My father bends over and kisses her. It is their first night apart since they've been married. She plays with the stuffed dog and laughs like a child. I kiss her good night. She reminds me to make her Jell-O; I smile. I feel tears welling inside of me. *She is so vulnerable,* I think, *and she needs me so much right now, but I am too afraid.* I will see her tomorrow. She will be okay. The preliminary tests look good.

We stand at the door, wave good-bye, and then head down the hallway. The tears run down my cheeks. I scold myself; I need to be strong. I want to turn back and tell her how important she is to me, but the nurses are already in the room checking her. I hate myself at this moment. She needs me, and I have let her down. I have missed another chance to tell my mother what she means to me. Maybe tomorrow I will tell her. I turn my head so my tears aren't visible to my father.

On the drive home, we talk about who will win the election. The conversation is annoying because all I can think about is what I should have said to my mother. When we arrive home, I sense something is not right. She will be home soon, maybe even tomorrow. I go to the kitchen and boil the water for her Jell-O.

Kelly Jean Laubenheimer

The Greatest Man

It doesn't matter who my father was. It matters who I remember he was.

Anne Sexton

My heart was pounding, my palms were sweating, and my breathing was heavy. The doctor had just walked into my hospital room with the cure for my spinal meningitis. It was a needle, the biggest one I'd ever seen, and all I could do was stare in disbelief. I was going to have a spinal tap, and although I had no idea what was going to happen, I knew just looking at the size of the needle that it couldn't be good. I wanted to run away, but my legs were too weak, and all I could do was lie there and watch him sanitize the gigantic needle. I was scared to death and wished all my pain would just go away.

And then it was like my wish came true. The most handsome, most caring man in the entire world walked into my room, and in that instant, I knew everything would be okay. His brown eyes and dark-brown hair looked all too familiar. "Daddy!" I cried, and he ran to me. As gently as he could, he hugged my exhausted body.

"Everything will be okay, Andrea," he told me. And then he said something I will never forget. He told me I needed to beat this so that I could stay around and be his little girl. He changed my life that moment he told me how he loved me with all his heart, and that I was the most precious gift he'd ever received. Having said that, my dad, a man I thought was stronger than steel, began to cry. And I don't mean just a few tears—he began to weep. I didn't know what to do.

"Don't cry, Daddy," I said, putting my aching hand on his shoulder and realizing that I needed to beat this disease. So, after he left, I calmly let the doctor insert the needle. The pain was like knives cutting into my skin, but the thought of how much my dad cared seemed to make everything go away. Since that moment, I have realized how much my dad means to me.

Looking back, I realize that I not only gained a better relationship with my dad that moment, but a friendship to last me a lifetime. My dad is always there for me, and always willing to listen. I never feel judged, and I know how much he cares. He is a great man. He isn't a world leader, a war hero, or a sports figure, but he is one of the greatest men who ever lived, and he will always be my hero!

Andrea Nickerson

Fake

We are what we believe we are.

Benjamin N. Cardozo

My mother trusted me when I told her I didn't smoke, even after she found a pack of cigarettes in my desk drawer. I didn't trust her when she said that the only reason she was going through my desk was to find some tape.

She didn't get mad when I tore my second contact lens in six weeks. She didn't even question me when I told her I borrowed her favorite white sweater and spilled red nail polish on it. My mother just smiled her usual, lopsided smile and forgave me. But it took me two weeks before I forgave her for not buying that certain brand of wheat bread that I liked. I also found it unforgivable when she made me listen to her hillbilly rock music station, when we could have been listening to my favorite. I'm still convinced that she insisted I wear a helmet to all those ice-skating parties when I was six just to make me look like a fool. I'll never forget the way people crowded around me, asking why I was wearing a helmet. I would just tell them the truth: my mother made me.

For all these years, I've been wishing my mother didn't do all the things she did. That was before I met Valerie. It was her first summer at camp, while it was everyone else's sixth. Her hair was blonde with black roots, and she had a scar that ran across her forehead.

At night, everyone would sit in a circle and talk about everything. We would share anecdotes about boys, our parents, and friends. I told my famous story about how I had tried to dye my hair blonde, but my mother wouldn't let me because she didn't want me to become "fake." Everyone giggled at my exaggerated story except Valerie. She just ran her fingers through her bleached hair and smiled. When it was time for her story, she began to rub the scar on her forehead nervously. I couldn't take it any longer; I just had to ask how she got that scar. I blurted out my question, which was returned with a deep stare from Valerie's brown eyes.

"I was ice skating and . . ."

I didn't even hear the end of her story. I just smiled to myself as I remembered those ice-skating parties. Everyone would give me such harsh looks as tears ran down my face. I also remembered staring in the mirror at my boring brown hair, listening to my mother tell me, "At least you're not 'fake.'"

Bonnie Tamarin

Happy with Nothing

Man's homeland is wherever he prospers.

Aristophanes

I once read a quote whose words captured my heart. "Life's an adventure," it said, before demanding to know, "What have you discovered?" It was funny how just a few words could get me thinking about my life.

Life truly is an adventure. When I was in third grade, my parents divorced. Even though I was young, I knew they could not love each other anymore. I don't remember my exact feelings, but I do know the hardships my mother, little brother, and sister, and I experienced as a result. My mom left that house knowing we wouldn't return. With nowhere to go, little education, a low-paying job, and three kids, I can't imagine the pressure and responsibility she felt. What courage she displayed!

I remember my mother was always calm. If she had any weakness, she made sure it didn't show through her perfect smile. Her actions and beautiful face always stayed hopeful and proud. To me, she didn't have a problem in the world. I remember the first time I saw her cry, years later. I was amazed. Tears. Actual tears. But back then she was a single mother with little in life except to protect her most precious possession—her children.

Without money, we couldn't buy or rent a home, so my mom's friend let us use her trailer. But this was not a normal trailer—subtract running water, electricity, and the bathroom. Yes, that's right, no toilet. But for some reason, none of that mattered because I was with my family.

Things then were different. I didn't need my hair dryer or my satellite dish; I had my most prized possession, my family. Even though our temporary home was small and our only neighbors were local boys and girls, we made the best of it. Things were cozy, fun, relaxing.

Every few days, we'd take a bath in a water trough. We'd pump the water from outside and boil it on the wood-burning stove. Then it would be taken to the middle of the living room, where our "tub" awaited! The bathroom was nothing but an outhouse. The only knowledge I got from the world came from my radio/CD player. I had one CD, and I lived off the music: Don McLean's *American Pie*. I knew every song, every word. It was our "family song." The moment *American Pie* blared from the speaker, all conversation stopped. We even had facial expressions and different tones of voices for the different songs.

Although I did not know it then, that experience taught me a lot. We had nothing, but we were happy. The good old days. A carefree girl in a giant world. Today, I can't imagine living in a house without heat or air conditioning. I can't believe I once didn't have a bathtub, toilet, or kitchen sink. I look back and realize I was just as happy, maybe even happier than now, even though I had next to nothing. I am always grateful for what I have and for the family I have been blessed with because my trip through life has been a bumpy ride!

Life is a lesson, an adventure, a new door urging you to

go through. Throughout life, you learn so much about those around you, and also about who you will become. I know my life has just begun, and already I feel I've discovered so much more than I could have imagined. This story shows the value of family and how important it is in time of need. So far in my life adventure, I have discovered my love for my family and especially my mother. Without her determination and willpower, I don't know where my humble family would be. Today I've discovered much more about my family and myself through my mother's eyes.

Clair Saeger

Dear Mom and Dad

A tree cannot stand without its roots.

Zairian Proverb

I bet you think you understand me pretty well. You know my favorite foods, colors, and hobbies. You know my moods, mannerisms, and weaknesses. You even know what makes me overflow with excitement and what makes me so angry I could explode. Only you have seen me at my best—and my worst. But what you don't know is how much I love you, because I've never let you know. Why, I'm not sure. Maybe I was too shy, or too worried you would shun my sappy emotions; maybe I was just scared. That's not important now. You—Dad and Mom— are important now. And so I think the greatest gift I can give both of you at this point, a time when we have so few years left together, is my love and sincerest thanks for all you've done for me because you care.

Dad, throughout my fifteen years, you have blessed me with your strong and dependable presence, as well as your little acts of love and kindness that have so long gone seemingly unnoticed. You probably don't realize how much I appreciate all the things you do, like making juice and shaved ice when I'm sick. Thank you for always making sure I'm comfortable, not too hot or too cold, and for covering me with a blanket when I fall asleep in the car.

Also, I love when you bring home goodies from work simply because you feel like it. I greatly appreciate when you leave the lights on after everyone has gone to bed except me, because you know how much I hate to walk through the halls in the dark.

You have taught me how to build furniture, plant flowers, hang moulding, and fix a flat tire. More important, you have taught me to be practical, reliable, hardworking, loyal, and devoted to family. Some of my fondest memories are the times you let loose and acted like a kid again. I will never forget our cannonball contests off the diving board, or when you jumped with me on the trampoline.

I think the most important thing you have done is tell me you love me—not just once in a while, but every night before I go to bed. Some may think this makes the phrase lose its meaning, but I think saying it often actually deepens the message, as well as our relationship. All these things you do are incredibly important, Dad, and I hope one day I can show my child the same love and care.

Mom, you are a true inspiration because of your many selfless acts and amazing patience. You have always been there for me, no matter what. I will never forget when my secret sister forgot to buy me presents, and you bought a CD I'd really wanted, so I wouldn't feel left out. You've always stood firm through my mood swings and understood the difficulties that come with being a teenager.

One of my favorite things, Mom, is the way you hug. No one can give a big, cuddly, comforting hug like you. Even though you lead a very busy life, you have always found time to help me. You never complain about editing my papers, hemming my clothes, or chauffeuring me everywhere. You support me and try to give me opportunities you never had. Perhaps you think I don't notice all the sacrifices you make for your daughters and husband, but I do. I may never understand how great these sacrifices are to you, but your loyalty, love, and dedication are rare qualities that I admire more than you can ever know.

I suppose all that's left to say is thank you for providing for me, caring for me, teaching me, and most important, loving me. You have done so many things that touch me deeply, and I hope this letter will give you a glimpse into the boundless ocean that is my love for you.

Kimberly Williams

The God in My Father

My father never talked to me about how to treat people. Every act of kindness I have ever shown another person was because I was trying to imitate him.

Pamela McGrew

There is always a silence between my dad and me. Sometimes it is difficult to speak to him. He likes to read books; I like to watch TV. He wants me to concentrate on studying; I believe friends come first. Many times I go to my friends for advice and share my secrets with them. Sometimes I feel my friends are the ones who keep me alive, and my dad never understands that. But, most of all, he believes in Christianity, and I think religion is the root of evil.

We've had many hot debates over this that usually result in silence between us for days. I often say things that offend my dad and result in him sending me to my room. Sometimes I feel he loves God more than me, but then the sadness turns into anger, and I focus on hating God because of how much he means to my dad.

My dad always has an aura of humbleness. He treats people with respect even though they may have deceived him. He believes there is goodness in everyone. Often, he tells me, "Man is good in nature; to trust others is the first step to becoming a child of God." But I, a teenager who has seen the violence and mean intentions in my friends, have lost my faith in humankind.

Many times I have almost despised him for his naïveté. I felt far wiser and thus sometimes was ashamed to be his daughter. Or maybe I was jealous of his ability to bypass the curtains of self-interest and to be able to live in such a peaceful mind. But, for whatever reason, my sarcastic comments about my dad's religion continued. God was my dad's unhealed wound I could poke at whenever I was mad at him.

But one day I began to understand him. It was a day when I had friends over for a sleepover. My dad called me upstairs. I walked up unwillingly, thinking about the fun I was having with my friends. Then he told me that my grandfather had died. I was frozen in shock. My grandfather was in perfect health, and just two months before had told me he was coming to visit from China. The thought of never seeing him again was unbearable.

Then I looked at my dad. His eyes were filled with agony and guilt. He had spent most of his life in the United States during my grandfather's old age. In China it is customary for the son to care for his parents, but my dad had broken that custom.

I walked to my dad to attempt to comfort him and hugged him for a very long time. Then I heard the voices of my friends. They said the best part of the movie was coming, but everything happening downstairs now seemed irrelevant. My dad turned to me and said, "Go, they need you down there." I shook my head and said I wanted to sit beside him. He told me he wanted to be alone and that he would be fine. I left him and went to seek peace and comfort from my friends.

Before I went to sleep, I knocked on my dad's door and saw that he was praying. Suddenly, I understood God in his mind. God gives him guidance and a place to seek advice. He is almost like a friend who will never deceive him; my dad had found peace and comfort from God. That night I prayed with him and prayed for my grandfather.

Annie Xu

Portrait of My Brother

The first time I met him,
I was two years old.
His head was as bare
As the body of a newborn gerbil.
His eyes were big and brown
and stared back up at me.
I thought I was looking
Into the eyes of a puppy.
His face was as bright
As the sunrise on a May morning
when the morning mist has cleared,
and I can see olive-green leaves on the sleeping trees.
His miniature hands reached out,
clutching the ends of my chestnut hair,
yanking each strand.
His small fingers and little toes
were still pinkish,
sensitive to the touch of caring hands.
His mouth
made soft gurgling noises,
and little bubbles
formed on the edge of his lips.

Katie Weiss

Wedding Pictures

*When there is great love, there are always
miracles.*

Willa Carter

"I'm short. When I am no smart, I have nothing special."
I knew my mother was relaying her few words of wisdom,
but I kept my eyes on the supermarket meatball she had
put on my dinner plate.

"Your dad love his college. He find out that he like
research. I have bad college. I did not find what I like. I still
do not know." Searching for her tears, I raised my eyes
from the meatball to hers. She smiled.

As I cut my meatball into thin slices, I could only focus
on all the mistakes in her grammar. I was not ready for one
of the mother-daughter chats I once desired.

"But like I say yesterday, I look back, and I have good
life. God bless me so many ways. I should not feel bad. I
just feel like I didn't do anything." She smiled again.

My eyes moved to the bowl of tortellini between us. It
was filled with spaghetti sauce, meatballs, and green peas.

It looked like a repulsive combination of leftovers, which is exactly what it was. Next to the bowl, the gray pot of rice seemed out of place. My mother viewed rice as a staple: a meal was not complete without vegetables, fruit, and rice. On her plate, the rice was mixed right in with the tortellini concoction.

The silence that normally characterized dinner without Dad resumed. Seven-minute dinner, plate in sink, homework time. I glanced at the clock and prepared for my retreat. But before I could move, my mother decided to impart more of her ungrammatical knowledge.

"My sister, the one who . . ." my mother looked as if she wouldn't be able to say the word "died." I nodded.

"She was so pretty." Impatience began to rise, and I rolled my eyes. Couldn't she think of anything to say besides the fact that her sister was pretty? Physical appearances are not that important. She said the same thing last year when my cousin died of heart problems.

"She died of drug. We didn't really have drug like now. She sniff, what you say, something like glue," she said, more to herself than to me.

"No kidding?" I had always thought she died of some disease.

I looked at my mother again: her white shirt, short hair, plastic glasses. I saw her often, talked with her less. She had told me little about her life. Well, I had never asked. I had viewed her as a person I would never become. I never bothered to find out why she had gone from the top of her class at college and a woman on top of the world to one who spent a lifetime cooking meatballs and cleaning the kitchen floor. My curiosity about her had grown. Perhaps I was searching for an explanation for her depression. Perhaps I was frightened because I was slowly learning I was more like my mother than I'd ever imagined.

After leaving my plate in the sink, I went upstairs and

pulled out a photo album from underneath the road maps and old Bibles. The cover was stamped with orange and brown flowers, the binding undone. Although I could not recall looking through it, I knew it was their wedding pictures.

I laughed. There was Dad, skinny as ever, with the same mocking expression. And there was my mother. She was wearing a strapless yellow dress and platform shoes. She was smiling, but with an expression I had never seen. It had spirit.

"Am I pretty?" My mother stood behind me. She was. I nodded. "I told you. See? I was pretty."

She pointed to a close-up of her face. "I really not that pretty. I had one of the best makeup person in the country. See? I ask for light makeup. At that time, most people wear dark. You see how light that is, looks natural." She pointed to the yellow-dress picture. "I look more like that." I said nothing. I thought she looked much prettier in the yellow-dress picture.

"You should know my family," she said.

I was much closer to my father's side and knew only one of my mother's sisters. She had given me the stuffed-to-ripping Hello Kitty wallet I carried around to the dismay of my more sophisticated friends.

"This is Grandma."

My grandma seemed so different from the person who called once in a while for my mother. I hadn't seen her in eight years, and there were no pictures of her on our walls. Grandma looked chubbier and less fragile than I had imagined.

"Grandpa." I remembered him even less. I recently learned he had divorced my grandma. Though he seemed like the bad guy of the family, my mother sympathized with him.

"How old were you when they got divorced?" I asked.

"I had just come to America." My mother came here

after college; I figured her parents had divorced when they were about sixty.

My mother pointed to her sister (the one who gave me the wallet) and her brother. Then she pointed to a girl in a blue plaid dress with straight hair that fell just above her mouth. She must have been about thirteen. I stared at the girl—it had to be the youngest sister, the one who died at nineteen. I'd spent one summer with her daughter, who had been adopted by one of the other faces in the picture. A whole summer, and I just passed her by as some relative. I wondered if my brother had ever asked about my mother's sister. Was he as oblivious as me?

The last page had four pictures, but my eyes were drawn to a dark one in the bottom left corner. My father and mother stood with glasses of wine. My mother was laughing. Around her neck was a Victorian choker.

My throat tightened, and I couldn't hear a word my mother was saying. I kept staring at the choker—its dark velvet, ivory stone, rose bead. It was the same choker my mother had kept for twenty-five years. It was the same choker I had taken out of her drawer, unaware of its history. It was the same choker I had lost one day—and never found.

"And that's the pictures," I heard my mother say. I smiled at her. When words fail, I have learned to smile.

"Goody, goody?" my mother asked.

"Goody, goody," I replied.

I watched my mom leave the room. And then, staring at that lost choker, I began to cry.

Jessica Lin

7

THROUGH THE GENERATIONS

It is in the shelter of each other that people live.

Irish Proverb

Holding On

We loaded the car to visit every summer—
four animated girls were enough to leave you out of
    breath.
You won me with a Mickey Mouse ice-cream pop.
I won you with a mug made of Carolina red clay.
We cut out construction-paper hearts
and sent them to you with our love.
You cherished them all
because you knew that things would change.
Things would grow older.

When I got older, we drove down for a brief visit.
I noticed your hands shaking as you cut your meat,
your voice trembling as you quietly spoke.
You still had pink construction paper piled in your drawers.
But I didn't have time for paper hearts anymore.
You bought me a Mickey Mouse ice-cream pop.
But I didn't eat ice cream anymore.
But now, Granddaddy, if you could only
    buy me one more pop,
I'd eat it just for you,
to pretend that things hadn't changed

the way you knew they would,
and to love you as I did then, and as I do now—
both at once.

Because now I realize that you were just holding on
to the hand of a little girl who was too young
    to hold on with you.
And now that I understand,
that little girl has long since run off, out of sight.
And now that I understand,
it is suddenly my turn to do the holding.
So here's my hand, Granddaddy,

Hold on.

Kaidi Stroud

Her Gift

Where we love is home, home that our feet may leave, but not our hearts.

Oliver Wendell Holmes

"You've never been here before!" my mom said with a sharp, new edge to her voice. Even though these words were directed to my grandmother sitting next to me in the back seat, my head snapped up at the tone. In the instant that I met my mother's eyes, I remembered the talk we had when I was nine and found out that my grandmother had Alzheimer's disease.

Back then it was just another mysterious disease that did not have an effect on my life. I rarely saw my grandmother. Even though I knew there was something wrong when my parents sat me down and had a serious talk about her illness, the information went in one ear and out the other. It did not seem real, and, therefore, I considered my grandma's ailment as just another bit of news to be shoveled back into the compartment of my mind where I keep those things that are imaginary. But my mother's voice and the look in her eyes suddenly illuminated that compartment. Reality now upset my imagination.

Here we were, four years later, traveling along Route 91 on our way back from the beach house my parents had rented for a week, perhaps the last vacation my grandmother would be well enough to spend with us. Since my grandma was the smallest one in the car, she sat in between my friend Ross and me. Every now and then she would look over at me, and I would give her a wink and a smile, which she returned.

Ross was a little nervous around Grandma because she kept asking the same questions again and again. Although he smiled, it looked more like a nervous grimace. Everyone should have been in a laid-back, let's-take-a-break-from-everyday-life mode, but it was like we were traveling with a new exchange student, someone who no longer spoke our language. The best way to communicate with her was through the eyes and through laughter. Actually, I was enjoying her new don't-sweat-the-details way of looking at life. She had a funny laugh and was behaving like a mischievous little brother.

When Grandma saw the sailboats in the harbor, her wrinkled face relaxed, and she looked like the young schoolgirl she must have once been. Overcome with glee, she exclaimed, "I remember when I was here before." This was the comment that evoked the sharp response from my mother. I immediately flushed with anger at my mother's voice, but when I looked in her eyes I saw more than anger; I saw her frustration at seeing her mother, the woman she looked up to her whole life, losing ground, and fear of everything that must be faced in the future. Even though my mother only paused momentarily before taking charge in her lawyerlike fashion, I saw in that silence a need I could fill. I could build a bridge and, in so doing, cross into adulthood, as I allowed my grandmother to ease back into innocence. The process would help us all.

Realizing my mother and grandmother had reached uncharted water, I threw them a line. I asked Grandma what her favorite seafood was. Once again, her eyes brightened, and she licked her lips with new appetite. She asked me if we could stop somewhere to eat lobster. I nodded enthusiastically, and any discomfort Grandma felt from her verbal exchange with Mom was completely erased as easily as erasing chalk off a blackboard. I quickly filled the blank board with new facts and equations, ignoring the fact that these, too, would be erased from Grandma's memory, possibly forever.

My grandmother died two years later, but she left me a valuable gift. For the first time, I had faced a difficult situation on equal footing with my parents, and Grandma's smile and wit encouraged me to take the lead.

Andrew G. Briggs

Gram

At eighty-four, the old girl's soul
is ripe and tart like wine,
filling her dank and musty body
like a forgotten cellar.
Sitting in a chewed blue armchair all day
makes her a tight wad of nerves.
Her wild eyes dance maniacally behind useless panes;
her flaming tongue spurts senseless, spicy words
at people passing.
She is a queen, that little dragon lady,
a queen on a threadbare throne.
But that suits me just fine;
to me she's as darling as a restless child
watching a wet, white snowfall
smother the playground in December.

Susan Landry

Big Hollow Middle School
26051 W. Nippersink Rd.
Ingleside, IL 60041

Christmas Cookies

To love and be loved is to feel the sun from both sides.

David Discott

"Are we there yet?" asked a sleepy voice from the back of the dark car. It was the tenth time my little sister had asked. Sadly, I had been counting. Long and bumpy car rides from New York to Ohio aren't exactly exciting. The only thought that kept us all from mutiny was knowing we were going to a place we dearly loved.

We went to Grandpa and Grandma's for Christmas for as long as I can remember. Christmas at home barely felt like Christmas. My mom spent her childhood there, remaining there until the day she said "I do" to my dad. Theirs was a small town, our second home, and we loved its sleepy atmosphere.

As we pulled into the driveway, I could already feel the warm glow that enveloped the house at Christmas time. In the front yard was Grandpa's annual light display, with the large wooden nativity painted in bright colors. There was no snow, which was disappointing, but what the house held was most important to us.

Grandpa came out first, as always. "How are my grand-kids?" he asked loudly and happily.

"I can't move my legs!" groaned my youngest sister.

Grandpa ceremoniously hugged us all, youngest to old-est, as he did every year. The air was filled with cries of "We're so glad to be here," and "My, my, how much you've grown!"

Tiredness faded. It was official. It was finally Christmas.

"No one goes in empty-handed!" yelled Dad. We grabbed our bags and pillows from the car and went inside to the family room, which was always warm and inviting. Colored lights were strung, and in the middle of the room the Christmas tree glowed; every shadow was deepened, every detail softened. An old, fuzzy-sounding Christmas record played on the stereo—perhaps Bing Crosby. This room was magical.

In the dining room, another smell emerged. Grandma had been baking again! But that was no surprise. We always found her there, always with something ready—maybe her Spanish chicken and rice. If we were really lucky it would be spaghetti with meatballs.

Mom always got the first hug from Grandma. They had a special mother-daughter moment we never intruded on. Then it was our turn: we all got a loving hug. We talked about school and the trip. Then Mom joined her for their cooking session. We knew all too well where Mom's cook-ing genes came from, although the prestigious position of "best family cook" came with age and experience.

Grandma was of medium height, thin with deep chocolate-brown eyes. Her hair was short and curly; my mom called it "salt and pepper." She wore grandmotherly clothes—pastel sweatshirts with flowers and matching pants. Grandma had a sweet voice and was always ready when you needed to have a good talk. She got up early every day to go to church with Grandpa and could often be seen saying the rosary.

I always thought Grandma was quiet. She wasn't shy but rather waited until it was her turn, always thinking before she spoke. I rarely remember her raising her voice, but, boy, if she did, you knew you had really done it. Grandma, at rare and special moments, could be funny. Her jokes were few and far between, but whenever she told one, we laughed.

Grandma spent most of her time in the kitchen. She would stay home and cook while we went downtown to skate or see the elaborate holiday train display. It was hard to believe such heavenly food came from that humble kitchen. Grandma was a miracle worker.

Of all the food from that ancient oven, the best was Grandma's Christmas cookies. After dinner we could choose two from her vast selection. These decisions were among the hardest of my life. There were the green, buttery wreaths and Christmas trees that were oh-so-crumbly and melted in your mouth. And her large and chewy sugar cookies with the extra-large Hershey's kiss in the middle that I always saved for last. There were butterscotch ones and perfect peanut-butter cookies with the traditional crisscross. And, of course, my personal favorite: the chewy candy canes with the minty icing and cute pink stripes. Grandma, always caring, would make plates of cookies we would deliver to her neighbors.

Christmas wasn't Christmas without being there, or having Grandma's Christmas cookies. But I knew—everyone in my family knew—that Grandma had cancer. I tried not to believe. It was easy at Christmas to deny anything was wrong. As all my aunts, uncles, and cousins opened presents that year, it was blissful. When Grandma received a warm robe from Grandpa, she held it up for the family to admire, her smile shining brightly.

I dreamed of Christmases past—and Christmases to come.

That was her last Christmas. Grandma died two months later. It was so sudden. I thought she had more time, and so did she. She left many things unfinished, cookies unbaked.

It was a shock when I visited her just before she died. She had been so different at Christmas from the half-delirious woman suffering in bed. Near the end, I knew she was ready. I'm sure she went straight to heaven. I bet she bakes cookies for the angels now.

Last Christmas was our first without her. During the long car drive I wondered if Christmas would ever be Christmas again. As we entered the family room everything seemed the same. Grandpa gave us warm, comforting hugs, just like always, youngest to oldest.

When we went into the dining room, however, it was clear something was missing. No one greeted us when we entered the old kitchen. There were no smells of Christmas cookies.

Grandpa pulled out a tin and offered us a cookie, but they were not the same. He had made slice-and-bake cookies—the kind with green trees and red snowmen in the middle. It was so sweet of him. He meant well. It made me want to cry.

"Boy," Grandpa joked between mouthfuls, "I'm sure glad I stayed home all day to make these."

And we all laughed. But I couldn't help thinking, *Grandma would have done that.* She would have labored over that ancient oven again this year. I knew Grandpa felt it too. He loved her so much. And now he missed her so much. If eating these cookies would give my grandpa comfort, I would eat a whole bathtub full. At least my mom baked some of our old favorites. At a too-young age, she assumed the title of "best family cook."

In the dining room was a new display: a photograph of Grandma as a beautiful Navy nurse with white candles burning bright next to white flowers. I gazed at it and thought of her and prayed for her and remembered . . . and the light aroma of freshly baked Christmas cookies gently surrounded me. Christmas had finally arrived.

Helen Comber

"Spoiling him? How can you say that?"

Reprinted by permission of Mike Shapiro. ©2007 Mike Shapiro.

When Grandparents Laugh

Beautiful young people are accidents of nature,
but beautiful old people are works of art.

Eleanor Roosevelt

I like Florida. And I don't like it just because it's hot, or because there are beaches, or because everyone goes there in the winter. I like Florida because there's something oddly comforting about curly, white-haired grandmas and potbellied, balding grandfathers riding three-speed bikes over rickety bridges. They dominate the beaches, those old men with missing teeth and old women with sloppy bright-pink lipstick smeared carelessly, obsessed with their bridge games, a sea of wrinkled, smiling faces half-hidden behind books, dragging their toes in the sand.

When it's hottest, around noon, they sometimes go down to the water. They grin and comment on the icy waves and hold each other's hands and walk side by side with their thighs slapping. Sometimes you can see the women power walking on the boardwalks or bike paths. Sometimes they drag their unwilling husbands along. The grandpas put on acts and pretend to hate walking and say they only want to sit and read or sleep and complain about aches in their backs. But the grandmothers and I, we know better. Our sweet, old men, our bald, toothless friends, enjoy walking.

When grandparents laugh, it's genuine laughter, and the sound is full and filled with mirth that is curiously real. Their clothes are loose and cool. Their smiles are very warm and extend to their eyes.

Grandparents are beautiful, especially when they're with their grandchildren. Their faces light up, and smiles double in size and brightness. They seem to radiate a pride and love that is rare, and known only to grandparents and me. They glow with satisfaction, for their grandchildren satisfy them.

Little pink bundles of baby, soft masses of damp curls on a toddler taking his first steps, a five-year-old with rosy cheeks learning to read, a third-grader mastering long division, boys entering middle school, and girls starting high school, proms and graduations and grandchildren going off to college—these are the people responsible for the shining beauty, the glowing love, the radiant pride of the grandparents.

Mariel Boyarsky

"Gramps, I told you riding the 'Killer Car' would be fun."

My Pepere

As I peer around the plants, I scan the field with eyes squinting from the brilliant sun. Seeing no one, I pop three deliciously sweet strawberries into my mouth, savoring each one. Then I stand and begin to search for the next inviting plant but find that I have devoured every one of the "perfect" strawberries. Deciding to change spots, I see him—a tall, husky man kneeling on one knee, his balding head covered with a hat and his eyes hidden behind sunglasses. I watch him. Drops of sweat bead on his face. The sun is beginning to be too much for him. He is amazing as he picks each strawberry with a precision only he possesses. Within a fraction of a second, he is able to tell the most scrumptious berries.

I trot over and proudly show him my bucket, which is half full. He smiles with approval. I feel good until I glance at his bucket, which is practically overflowing.

I pop a few more strawberries in my mouth, and he says, "Well, that should do it." Once we have our berries weighed, he hands the clerk the money with large, wrinkled hands. I race him to the car. He does not run, and it doesn't matter. We begin the long journey home. There is no music, and not much is said, yet the silence is welcomed. I glance at the man sitting next to me and wonder how old he is. In my childish mind, I imagine ninety, at least. He senses me staring, turns to me, and smiles. Ahh, that smile. It is one in a million. Through his smile, you can see it all. The warmth and love this great man possesses is startling.

Strawberry picking used to be an annual event. It was always sad to see the berry season end. Today the sun doesn't seem to shine as brightly, and it looks as if we won't go strawberry picking together this year. I am much older now, and so is he. Right now, I am not with that great man; I am with my sister on the way to see him. We walk through the revolving doors, down the hall, and to the elevators. His room number is E205. We walk briskly down another hall and around the corner and slowly walk through his door. I see him lying in an all-white bed with tubes coming out everywhere. He no longer looks like the man I went strawberry picking with. Now, he looks like a defenseless, old man whose health is beginning to fail.

"Hi, Pepere," I say. In almost a whisper, he replies, "Hello, Angie." I don't ask how he's doing because, honestly, I don't want to know. I look at him and say nothing. My mother and grandmother are there, too. He is doing his best to make conversation, but no one is sure of what to say. For me, I feel as if I am in a dream. It seems utterly impossible for such an awesome man to become so helpless. It's terrifying.

After a short time, we must leave. I kiss him good-bye and tell him I love him. Reluctantly, I go. We get in the car for the journey home. There is no music, and not much is said, yet the silence is deafening and painful. I throw in a tape and crank up the radio, hoping to drown out the pain I am feeling.

Good night, Pepere.

Angie Forest

She Said

My mother said, Nana
is sick.
I said nothing.
She said Nana
had a stroke last night.
I said nothing.
She said Nana is in
the hospital, dying.
I said nothing.
She said Nana is in a coma.
I said, with my eyes stiff and my heart numb,
nothing.
She said, she would want you to come
and see her one last time.
I said
nothing.
She lowered herself to my child's
eye level, looked into my shocked face,
into my blank mind, at my short gasps
for air, and said nothing.
I looked right into the whites of her eyes.
She began to cry.
I said nothing.
I wish I had said something.
There was nothing to say.

Katherine Cincotta

Visiting Hours Are Over

Life is ours to be spent not to be saved.

D. H. Lawrence

I stared at the hand intertwined with mine. Paper-thin skin and bony fingers. A ring, once shining new, now old, the band wearing away. She could barely hold on, but she did. I'm not sure what she was afraid of; there are so many things to fear, and yet nothing at all. We'd hoped she'd get better, but she was old, so old, and we were giving up hope. So was she. She was giving up everything.

We were alone in that dim room, the curtains half-drawn but the door open. It seems more appropriate to say that I was alone in that dim room; she hadn't said a word for so long. I felt out of place, scared. The cold somehow crept in through the window. It slid through the pores of my skin, worked into my bones. I felt frozen to my seat. All I could think was, *Damn the cold.*

I waited. I waited for the minutes to pass. I waited for my mother to come back. I waited for this old woman to say something, anything. And when she did, I wanted to plug my ears and turn away.

She told me it hurt. She never said what, she just kept telling me it hurt, that the pain was too much, help her, save her.

I didn't know what to say. My instinct was to squeeze her hand a little tighter, to tell her everything would be okay. *Tell me what's wrong, and we'll make it all right.* But I couldn't. I was afraid my own bony fingers would turn into razors and cut her delicate skin; I was afraid they would become lead and crush her delicate bones. I was afraid to lie to her, because I knew things would not be okay anymore.

Okay? How does one define okay? Things were okay when this woman had let me beat her at cards or checkers. Things were okay when she made me pray the rosary every day with her. I haven't prayed in a long time, and those cards are so creased and bent at the corners, they would tear now.

I had no choice. I lied. I told her everything would be okay. *Tell me what is wrong, and we'll make it all right.* I don't think she heard me, though. At least, not really. But she did calm down enough so I could talk her into taking some painkillers. After two months of a strange paranoia that "they" were out to get her, to poison her, she trusted only me.

I half-expected the nurse to cry, she praised me so much. The more plaudits I got, the more shame I felt. I felt like a traitor. I felt like I'd sided with the enemy—at least, in this woman's half-closed eyes.

And when those brown-eyes-turned-gray-with-age closed completely, I never felt more scared. There was one thought that even the coldness of the room couldn't penetrate: I would never see her alive again. I gave her hand the tiniest squeeze. My final good-bye. I bit my lip and begged the Higher Power to let her open those eyes again, please, oh, please, wake up. I watched her chest move up and down, slowly, steadily. A glance at the clock told me it was time to go—visiting hours were over.

I couldn't bring myself to look back. It was too draining. After all, I was leaving a thousand and one little pieces of my life behind, right beside the greatest woman I'd ever known.

Megan Willman

Pancakes and Beethoven

My grandparents have a beautiful house in Cape Cod, with white trim, weathered shingles, and a red door. In front is a picket fence, and out back, a garden overflows with flowers of all shapes and colors. At night, I sit on the deck with my brothers and sisters, stargazing and eating s'mores while soaking in the hot tub and letting the songs of Beethoven, Louis Armstrong, or Dave Matthews drift through my head.

Every summer, I found time to visit my grandparents. When high school began, though, I had little free time. The summers were spent working, and when I wasn't running around, I was babysitting or helping my mom around the house. I was left with little chance to socialize, and no time to spend with my grandparents.

Then, on my parents' anniversary, which conveniently falls in midsummer, I was instructed to take time off from work to go to the Cape with my brother and sister to spend the weekend with my grandparents. I went willingly, with thoughts of escaping my nine-to-five lifestyle, not of visiting.

When we pulled into the driveway early that Friday morning, there was, as usual, music playing on the deck.

After my parents left, my grandfather and I sat at the deck table. We each read a section of the newspaper as my grandmother bustled in the kitchen preparing German pancakes, a family favorite, with my sister and brother.

I poured a cup of coffee, adding the usual two sugars. "You are too young to drink coffee," my grandfather smirked from behind his paper. He took a sip of his.

"If I am too young," I replied, "then you are definitely too young." He chuckled. A new symphony blasted from the speakers. "Mozart?" I guessed.

"Actually, Beethoven," he said, folding his paper. "A brilliant man," my grandfather began and proceeded to discuss Beethoven's genius even after he went deaf.

Twenty minutes later, I was an expert on Beethoven, and with his "Moonlight Sonata" playing, I brought my coffee mug into the kitchen to greet my grandmother.

"Coffee?" she questioned, her eyebrows raised. I shrugged. "Well, the pancakes are almost ready." She took off her apron and examined her hands. She has beautiful hands. "How is the summer going?" she asked.

"Busy," I said with a dramatic eye roll, falling onto a kitchen stool.

"Don't get too overwhelmed, my dear," she said, putting her hand on my cheek and yanking a curl. "Plus, Grandpapa and I wanted to take you to see an opera at the little theater downtown." She pulled the orange juice— freshly squeezed—out of the refrigerator. "After breakfast, put on your bathing suit. The water is so warm this year."

"I believe it," I said. "I can't wait to be on the beach."

"But now, be honest with me. What do we think of my new haircut? Too short?"

"Just perfect," I assured her.

We took the pancakes out of the oven, all crisp on the outside and fluffy on the inside, and walked out to the porch to devour the early morning dessert, sprinkled with lemon and powdered sugar.

We spent the rest of the day lounging in the sand with feet buried, while the portable radio played. My grandmother sang along with Ella Fitzgerald as she put hummus on her cracker. She has a beautiful voice. My grandfather read aloud an article on the USS *Constitution* and somehow managed to segue into the fresh strawberries in the garden and the truth about the Cuban missile crisis.

Maybe it happened as I took a bite of the pancake at breakfast. Maybe it happened when I was looking through my grandmother's old photographs and she was critiquing her hair in the '50s. Maybe it was every time my grandfather called me "Toots." Maybe it happened as I watched the sky explode with reds and oranges and pinks as the sun set over the beach. But, at some point, I had an epiphany.

I will have many jobs, some I will like more than others. If the dishes are not loaded in the dishwasher and my bed is not made, life will go on. Working nine to five and folding socks are not the important things in my life. The important things are the people who love me unconditionally. Even friends will come and go, but I will always have this family who calls me Toots and phoned toy stores around the country to find the stuffed monkey I wanted when I was seven.

Sitting on a deck chair, eating pancakes, and listening to the history of the Hawaiian Islands with my grandparents, all while "Carmen" croons in the background—that is what matters.

Sarah Miles Ryan

They Say It's a Hospital

They say it's a hospital,
but I know better.
Visitors, holding carnation bouquets,
wear brightly colored T shirts, casual khaki shorts,
but their eyes are all glazed hard with worry,
their smiles are just brightly painted plastic.
The front desk attendants are chatty and careless, talking
about Sunday plans.
They call it a hospital,
but I know better.
He is calm now. The medications tape his pallid
One-hundred-and-fifty-three-pound body together. They
   kindly allow him to speak, but
not to hear. They allow him to maintain his wild delusions,
but not to listen to us.
They say it's a hospital,
but I know better.
He looks at my mother and says:
"I had twin puppies yesterday.
They took them away from me, though.
They put them in a place where only Marines could go.
And I tried to go there, but

They caught me. Isn't it nice that
They allow me to have visitors in jail?"
The photographs around him try to create a chorus
    of the familiar.
But they just depress me more. Who wants to remember
    that this man was once a gardener, father, husband?
    The nurses
alone can admire the photograph of his beautiful white
    country house.
"Fiona," he mumbles at my four-year-old sister,
    as she pulls herself closer to my mother's leg.
"Fiona, what a beautiful name for a beautiful child."
They call it saving a man's life,
But I know better.

Renata Silberblatt

8

FITTING IN

I know that the world is not filled with strangers. It is full of other people—waiting only to be spoken to.

Beth Day

Bubble Trouble

"Mrs. Jenson?" My teacher turns, her eyebrows raised and her lips drawn together to let me know that I am skating on thin ice asking a question during our final standardized test of the year.

"Yes, Valerie." The way she holds the final syllable in her mouth through slightly clenched teeth makes me hurry. "Umm . . . here in the box for race, is it okay if I bubble in two?" Mrs. Jenson gives me a pitying look (they always do) before consulting the test directions. "I'm sorry, sweetie, but the directions say mark only one." They always do; I guess I just like to mount a small protest. I shrug as we move painfully along through how to correctly mark our birth date, complete with the reminder that "You were not born on today's date." I suppose this is their own brand of standardized humor. I finish but go back to that little box marked "Race." I study how it lies near "Gender" and wonder if the people who designed these tests believed that in all the years to come, test-taking students of America could so easily break down their identity into two simple categories. Suddenly, we are moving on; I need to choose. Which part of me should I deny today?

I am not so easily squashed into one category. I am Eurasian. When I tell people this, they may say, "Oh! Where is Eurasia?" Or they think it is floating around somewhere near Malaysia or the Philippines or Sri Lanka or one of those countries they can never remember. So I say, "Actually, I'm half Asian and half Caucasian." To this, one girl responded, "Then aren't you Asian?"

Due to my dark hair and pale skin, people have assumed I am everything from white, Chinese, Japanese, Korean, Inuit, and, my favorite, Mexican (which explains why one friend kept pestering me about fajitas). I've never really minded because when people finally figure out my split family tree, they usually just say "Oh!" and keep talking. That's why I love living in such a great ethnic stew of a country.

What annoys me is that no matter where I turn, I'm confronted with people who speak like the bubbles, demanding, "Asian slash Pacific Islander, or Caucasian? We must know!" Once, during a team-building exercise, my little team got into a fierce debate over ethnicity. Since I speak fewer words of Chinese than an infant knows, the Chinese girl in my group insisted I was white.

"She can't be white; she looks too Chinese!" cried another. "I think you are what you look like!"

"What about you are who you are?" countered another.

"How about, 'I'm me. I'm two races. I embrace each equally, and I can't just fling one out the window because of the way you perceive me?'" I said, finally getting in a word. "What's it matter who I look like?"

"She's definitely Chinese."

"White!"

After more than a decade of methodically switching his race every other year, my brother threw up his hands and started marking two bubbles his last years of high school. I'm still too afraid to attempt something so bold for fear of messing up my test scores. (I guess that's the Chinese in me.) And what's with that "Other" bubble? My friends agree that it would just feel weird to put that down, like you're some sort of alien who snuck in. But what if your race isn't even listed? I really wish that students had more choices in marking those wretched little bubbles.

All I understand for certain is that my parents must really love each other to have braved the barriers and difficulties of merging two cultures. The least I should get is another bubble.

Valerie Gribben

The Longest Hallway

Remember always that you have not only the right to be an individual; you have an obligation to be one.

Eleanor Roosevelt

Most people I know like to have gym late in the day, so they aren't sweaty in all their classes. But I prefer it in the morning, so it's not hot when we're outside, and the bees aren't active. I was lucky this year because my schedule allowed me to have gym first period. My least favorite class would get over with early.

Today, Monday, is one of those ambiguous spring days. It is warm enough to wear shorts if I want to, but it might be better to wear pants. This is what I worry about as I say good-bye to my friends and leave homeroom. *Do I change into sweat pants, or wear shorts?* I don't forget to keep an eye out for Peter, but he must have gone the other way today.

The locker rooms aren't too far from my homeroom, but to get there I must walk down a hallway that stretches forever past the art rooms, cafeteria, and outside doors. I hate to walk it alone, but I have no choice. Three seniors, the kind of guys I can't picture as adults with jobs and families, lean against the wall to my right. I will not be afraid; they can't hurt me. I have trained myself to walk past them without making eye contact. I pick a spot farther down the hallway and stare at it. Eye contact with them is deadly. I would become a victim; I would become vulnerable.

I concentrate on walking, swinging my arms casually, and already I am past the first senior. Coming upon the second one, I fail. They have laughed, and I lose my focus point. Worse, I look at them, opening myself up for attack. It's too late to undo; I must wait for whatever they choose to heap on me. The middle kid, kind of goofy looking, smiles. I am almost relieved, can almost breathe again, but there is a little corner of me that remains wary. A smile means nothing in the hallways of this school.

That suspicious, scared little person inside of me is proven right. When I am a few feet beyond the last guy, I hear more laughter. My heart sinks, and I wait for the words, rather missiles. They come.

"Black Afro . . . frizzy head . . ." I do not hear the rest, but I don't need to. I have heard these words before, and they are no longer a shock. I am not angry. I feel no rage. No, I am sad, and worse, I am ashamed. I feel guilty for my shame, want to kill it, but still my face burns. No matter what I do—perms, curling irons, hot combs, curlers, hair gels—I cannot get my hair to lie flat. It is thick and wild. I want to tell that kid, the goofy-looking one, that he is wrong—it's not an Afro. But I don't turn around because I know that underneath these chemically treated curls, loathed and loved by me, the roots are already growing in, and that I will wait as long as possible before perming them again. Plus, I am late for gym class.

Kendra Lider-Johnson

The Fat Kid

If we really want to love, we must learn to forgive.

Mother Teresa

"Recess!" one boy yelled. Lines formed quickly, but I stayed at the end. Looking down, hands in my pockets, I kicked rocks across the blacktop. I watched the boys play basketball as the girls looked on. They did not know who I was. I wondered whether I should ask to play, but just then Joe hit the ground. He limped to the side of the court with help from a teammate.

"Hey, you want to play?" asked John, his team now short a man. John was a tall, skinny boy everyone liked. He was one of the most athletic kids in my grade.

"Umm, I'll play the next game," I said as I sat watching. That's all I ever did—watch.

The next day, science, math, social studies, and English passed as usual, and I sat with friends eating lunch.

"Are you going to play basketball with us today?" asked John. "Joe is still hurt."

"Yeah, I'll try it today," I said nervously, knowing what would happen.

Lunch ended, and the lines to go outside formed even faster than the day before. John called me to the hoop, and I walked over slowly, peering out of the corner of my eye at the girls watching. I saw one of them point at me, but I kept walking.

The game started, and everything was okay. I made a few baskets, and, as one of the tallest kids, I got a lot of rebounds. Although this was only recess basketball, I felt like I could play for the New York Knicks. The day was perfect, and after watching for all those hours, I was glad to finally play.

The girls came over. I tried not to make eye contact, but it was difficult not to. A group of them chanted "Fat @$$" and "Lard @$$," but I kept playing.

During the next period, I sat with my head on the desk. I didn't want those girls to know they'd gotten to me. I would laugh at anything just to put it out of my head. I kept hearing their words, though, and felt myself shatter completely.

I went home on the bus that day with my head leaning against the window. My mom was waiting at my stop. I walked to her and gave her a hug, sobbing. I told her they'd made fun of me again. I told her I wished I was thin, and that kids weren't so mean to me. Even though I did have friends, I felt like I didn't and never would because people saw me as fat before they got to know me.

I fell asleep that night wondering what it would be like if I were a skinny, handsome boy. I was jealous of all the kids who were never teased and had everything easy. No one I knew got teased the way I did. Maybe it was a good thing. *Maybe,* I thought, *maybe it will make me mellow when I grow up.* But now, I was the boy no girls ever looked at.

A few years later, I went to a sports camp with activities

every second we were awake. In the beginning, I was the same "fat kid" I was at school. But, week by week, the pounds came off. When my mom visited after five weeks, she couldn't get over how I looked and told me I must have dropped at least fifteen pounds. I felt great. Three years of camp passed, and I dropped more and more weight. Each summer I came home a different person.

One day at school, I saw an overweight boy walking through the hall with his head down, trying not to make eye contact. I thought that maybe he had been teased like I had been and just couldn't take it. I wondered if he was crying like I once had.

The next day, I saw him again.

"You're so fat!" yelled a boy.

"You're the fattest kid I've ever seen!" taunted another as he shoved him against the locker.

My good friends, ones I had known since I was little, were teasing this boy and calling him the same names that had traumatized me through the years. Upset, I went over to them.

"Get away from him!" I screamed. "What did he ever do to you?"

Although they walked away, I didn't think they got the message that words hurt. The boy looked at me, smiled, and said thanks, and then walked to his next class. He never looked back; he just kept walking through the hallway. This time, though, he walked with his head up.

David Gelbard

"So the teacher said 'anybody
with dyslexia raise your right hand.'"

Cooking with Fire

It is never too late to give up our prejudices.

Henry David Thoreau

He looked me up and down as I bent over with my farm-animal-print oven mitts. I gave him an irritated "What are you looking at?" stare. I stood up, pan in hands, turned, and kicked the oven door closed.

I looked at the tin of cupcakes with a smile. They were perfect. I could hear my father mutter something from where he was sitting at the dining room table.

"Did you say something?" I asked, looking over my shoulder. My father never liked to see me cook. He liked food, but seeing me be so domestic annoyed him. My father is one of the most conservative, arrogant, closed-minded men I know, and seeing his only son baking cupcakes on a nice summer day instead of playing football was not a sight he enjoyed.

"Don't you think baking cupcakes is a little . . ." his words trailed off, and I rolled my eyes as I prepared the frosting and sprinkles. I knew exactly what he wanted to say, but then he mustered up his courage.

"Don't you think it's a little . . . gay?" he asked, rather politely. It was the first time I had ever heard him use this word in a sentence. My mind was crowded with thoughts like, *Oh, no, who told him? I'm going to kill my sister! Why would my mother do that to me?* I pretended I hadn't heard him. I hadn't "outted" myself to my father yet and was really hoping to put it off forever.

"Did you hear me?" he asked. "Moritz, are you gay?"

My mind became overwhelmed with flashbacks of grade school when I had been persecuted for being energetic, sensitive, creative . . . gay.

I walked into the dining room, took a deep breath, and figured it was about time to tell my father. It's not like he didn't already know, right?

For the next hour and a half, I don't think I've ever said so much to my father. He was the kind of man I tried to avoid: pro-life, against gay marriage, and unreceptive to ideas other than his own. But now, he seemed different. He seemed to understand that I was a gay teenager. He seemed to accept the fact that I had told everyone but him. He seemed like someone I'd want to talk to. He seemed like the father I had dreamed of.

"It's okay to be who you are," he said. "I just want you to know that I'm still your father, and I'll always love you." I nodded and gave him a hug.

During our hug, I smelled my cooling cupcakes. I frosted them, and then we shared them.

That day I realized that my resentment toward him for being who he is didn't matter. He didn't care if I were gay, or if I hated him—he would always love me. I would always be his son, and he would always be my father.

He gave me some of the best advice ever: be who I am despite what others think. He gave me hope that even the most conventional, egotistical, and ignorant people can come around. I realized my father was still human and not some heartless robot. I realized he would not always approve of my decisions, but he would always support me.

"You know, I always knew," he said to me while picking at the cupcake.

"Oh," I said, not surprised at all.

"You know what else?" my father asked as he set down his cigarette and cupcake. "These would go great with chocolate milk."

Moritz Mathias

Becoming a Goth

Carrie, Amanda, and I headed for the mall. We talked about the same things we usually did, went to most of the same stores, and walked around in the same manner we ordinarily did. The only differences were our clothing and makeup.

We had become goths with simple adjustments to our appearance. Gothic, if you don't know it by name, is the mostly black, some red, chained garb that some people enjoy wearing. That day, Amanda was wearing a black skirt and top, black glasses, fishnets on her arms, striped knee socks, and black shoes. Her hair was atop her head in two buns. I wore a red plaid skirt, fishnet stockings on my legs and arms, knee-high black lace-up boots, a black sweatshirt, and headphones, and some of my hair was pink. I even wore a small red nose ring, which was undetectably fake. My eyes were thickly lined, and Amanda and I both wore black lipstick. Carrie sported an incredibly short black skirt, ripped black stockings, a low-cut plaid jacket with black fur trim, and a red sequined devil-horn headband. We were all adorned in chokers, rings, and multiple pairs of earrings.

When I looked in the mirror at my house, my first

thought was, *I'm liking this look. Why don't I dress like this more often?* But I knew why—this outfit made me look like I was begging for attention. It was the clothing of a different group of people, of which I would never be a part.

Entering the mall, we initially noticed only a few glances at our clothes. That was to be expected. Then there was some laughing and pointing. At one point, a whole family watched us. Some people, including adults, stared rather obnoxiously. A middle-aged man stopped beside us and gave a quiet "You're looking good" whistle. It didn't sound like a joke; it was rude—and serious. Our clothing made us seem less respectable.

As we walked through the mall, escalators full of people gawked at us. We found this rather funny most of the time, but once in a while our mouths fell open in astonishment at some of the ruder reactions. Some salespeople treated us the same, but in other stores they seemed disgusted by our attire. In a bookstore, Carrie asked for the poetry section. "It's in the corner, in the back," he told her elusively. She looked but found no poetry.

Later, we returned to the store after we had taken off our makeup and dressed in our normal jeans and shirts. This time we began looking at journals. An employee came over and showed us which journal was her favorite. After she left, Carrie nudged me and said, "That guy at the register was definitely checking us out."

"Where is the mystery section?" Carrie asked. This time he said, "Oh, let me show you." He then politely took her to the section. Looking around, I noticed the store was just as busy as it had been before. Obviously, our clothing affected some people's reactions to us.

At one point our gothic style had made a mother steer her kids away from us, and another lady had walked by with a look of utter disgust. As she passed, I heard a great, loathing sigh of disapproval. One lady commented, "Isn't that weird?" Her older companion replied, "I think it's cute." That was the best comment we heard all day.

We even passed three young military men. There are stereotypes that go with military men just as there are ones with goths. I expected the three to be stiff, but mostly respectful. That's why it surprised me when the man in the middle coughed and muttered "hoes" as he looked at us, and the other two laughed.

When it came time to change, I looked one last time in the mirror at an outfit I was beginning to enjoy, despite the comments. In some ways it was fun to get a rise out of people and see what they had to say. It amazed me that some seemed so mad when they had no idea who or what I really was.

Dressed in my usual clothing, I noticed an immediate change. I wasn't anything to anyone anymore, just another teenager roaming the mall. I was looking for people to stare at me in my blue jeans, but they didn't. I was looking for a whisper, a sign of my existence in someone's eyes, good or bad, but there wasn't any. One woman did stop and ask where a particular store was, and we politely told her as we would have in our other clothing, although I'm sure we never would have been asked dressed in our goth attire.

As we were leaving the mall, I noticed a short, overweight man in a funny little poncho and almost whispered to Amanda, "Look over there," but I stopped myself as I realized that he, too, had probably been followed by whispers and stares all day.

The moral of the story is heard many times, but I'll repeat it because a lot of people don't get it: don't judge people by the way they look. It's what is on the inside, not the outside, that counts.

Maria Adelmann

I'm Not Prejudiced, Am I?

If we were to wake up some morning and find that everyone was the same race, creed, and color, we would find some other cause for prejudice by noon.

George Aiken

I'm not prejudiced. I can't be. I was raised in a white upper-middle-class household in the suburbs in a little town of thirteen thousand. My parents had always reinforced the idea that all people, regardless of skin color, were equal. I had grown up on the "Sesame Street" scenes where Muppets of all colors played and lived together. Being a minority myself, I had always been sensitive to comments about race or religion and tried to get my friends to refrain from telling racist jokes, at least in front of me. I even remember teaching my younger sister, when only three years old, not to judge people by their looks. ("It doesn't matter if you play with someone with green or purple or brown skin, as long as they're fun.") So, it was pretty safe to conclude I'm not prejudiced.

Or so I thought.

One summer, I attended a program at Brown University where I met a variety of people: black, Asian, Haitian, Hispanic. It was a great experience, since there was little racial diversity at my high school. (Out of the 550 students, there were only ten blacks and an equal number of Asians and Jews; the remainder of the population was white and Christian.) I took a literature course where one section focused on the relationship between people and fear. We confronted issues of race, religion, and sexual preference, which make people different from each other, and thus, create fear. It was there that I first experienced conflicting feelings about race and my own thoughts.

An African-American girl, Lia, explained the experiences that she had had because of her color. Suddenly, a vicious thought came into my mind: *Am I perfectly innocent? Do I hold prejudices that I refuse to confront?* I had always tried to be the understanding liberal, the tolerant one who (supposedly) understands and sympathizes with all people. At that moment I remembered a conversation that I had had with my Hebrew tutor when asked the question: "If you were walking down a city street at night and saw a man walking toward you, would you be more frightened if the man were black instead of white?" At the time, I thought I was totally unbiased, and after grappling with the question, came to the conclusion that it wouldn't make a difference. I truly believed this, but my teacher remained incredulous. "We have a fear of the unknown," he said. "It's natural. We can't help it—it is human nature to fear that which is not like you. I suspect that, deep down, where you can't or won't look, you know who you would fear more." I didn't agree—I'm not prejudiced, remember?

But that fall as my mother drove me through a nearby city, I spotted three young black men. They seemed a bit "suspicious" to me, looking around as if to see if anyone was watching them. As we drove by, one reached into his sock and pulled out something small. "That was a drug deal we just saw!" I remarked, confidently. My mother turned and looked. "He gave the man a piece of gum. Juicy Fruit."

I was stunned. There I was—the unbiased, unprejudiced liberal—a racist. I had assumed that because they were young black men standing on the street corner, they had been exchanging drugs. I had made the assumption quickly, naturally. Without a doubt in my mind. Suddenly, I was forced to face my own racism.

What I'm trying to say is that all of us, no matter how hard we try not to be, are human. I realize now that I, like everyone, do fear that which is not like me. However, my realization does not make me cynical. Rather, it does the opposite. I now know that I am prejudiced, but, by recognizing this, I can at least hope to overcome it. I know who I am, and who I can become.

Aaron Shield

"Bud, could we talk about something besides the game last night. . . . I don't even like sports."

Still Me Inside

"I need a change!"

And so on that single whim, I cut my long black hair, streaked it bright red, and, to top it off, pierced my eyebrow. I had gone from dork to punk in a week, and as trivial as it seems, this transformation has had a great effect on my life.

As long as I can remember, I had always been a good girl. In school, I got decent grades and never was in trouble. At home, I tried not to give my parents too much grief. But more than that, I had the "look" of a good girl. People always stereotyped me as a quiet, studious, Asian girl. Friends' parents often asked if I played the violin or the piano. "No, the flute," I'd say, and they would nod, not surprised. Walking around with my long black hair over my face, I hid behind my stereotype. I felt somewhat obliged to appease the stereotype imposed on me.

Needless to say, heads turned the day I walked into school sporting a new, short, bright red hairdo. I enjoyed the reaction and attention I received from my friends and teachers. I didn't listen to my friends' warnings about people seeing me differently, people who frowned on a "rebellious punkster." After all, I was still the same person inside, so why should this change matter? I soon found out how naive I was.

One day, I was late for school and needed a pass from my vice principal. I was met by a surprisingly stern look. Writing one, his voice and stare were cold and condescending. Mistaking me for "one of those punk delinquents," he left me with a warning: "Don't make a habit of it." Had I come late to school a week before, my vice principal would have said nothing. I was not used to this discriminating treatment, and I felt angry, embarrassed, and somewhat defeated. Now every time I go to the mall, suspicious eyes follow me. Store clerks keep a cautious watch. But the worst was yet to come.

It was the night of our music recital for advanced students. For weeks, I had prepared my piece, and I was excited. The room was packed with parents waiting to hear their children. But, as soon as I walked into the room, all attention was focused on my head. As I sat waiting my turn, I felt the critical eyes of the parents.

I performed well but felt awful. Afterward, I still saw those disapproving looks as they walked out with their children. I even overheard a friend being lectured on how she shouldn't color her hair or pierce her face to become "a punk like Mai." Once again, I was ready to go home feeling angry when my friend's father stopped me.

"You were very good tonight. At first I didn't recognize you," he said, looking at my head.

"Oh, yes, I look very different from last time, don't I?"

"Well, you played even better than last year. Look forward to hearing you again."

I went home feeling good, as if I had finally won a battle. Now the stern look of the vice principal, the suspicious stares of the store clerks, and the disapproving eyes of my friends' mothers didn't bother me. I was still the same person inside, punk or not. There was nothing wrong with me; it was the other judgmental people who had the problem. I regained my confidence.

I still get looks and the stares, but it doesn't upset me. In a way, I traded in one stereotype for another, but this time I enjoy proving them wrong. People are surprised to see me getting good grades and applying to good colleges. They're surprised to hear me play the flute so well. And they are absolutely shocked to see me standing in front of the football field, red hair shining in the sun, conducting the marching band!

As for my red hair, I re-dye it occasionally to keep it bright, burning red. It seems to give me the power to fight against stereotypes forced on me and gives me the confidence that I never had before.

Mai Goda

More Than a Wheelchair

*S*ome things are better left unsaid.

George Bernard Shaw

People judge. That's a fact. They judge clothes and appearances, the outside of a person. Very few take the time to explore what's inside. I was guilty of this, too, until I really got to know my brother Bret. He has taught me the value of loving people for who they really are, even if they have a disability. I know I still judge too quickly, but I hope I don't as often.

Bret was born seven weeks early and weighed only three pounds. He was so small that his forearm was only as long as my mom's thumb. He has cerebral palsy, a condition that can be caused by lack of oxygen to the brain during childbirth.

One word many people use to describe Bret is "incapable." In fact, incapable is at the other end of the spectrum when I describe my brother. I would characterize him as witty, smart, fearless, courageous, spirited, and sometimes too independent, but definitely not incapable.

Bret has a tremendous memory. He rarely forgets a

name or date, even if he only overhears it. His sense of hearing is keen, especially when someone is talking about him. He knows almost everything about every sport and enjoys playing them on his computer. He loves telling jokes, going to concerts, watching television, and checking the answering machine as soon as he gets home. He's pretty much an ordinary teenager, although some don't see him that way.

When I go anywhere with him, people stare. They stare at his wheelchair, his spindly arms and legs that never seem to move, his crooked feet with his big toe curled under the others, and his S-shaped back that doesn't look very pleasant. When they hear him talk, they don't understand his slurred speech. Probably two thoughts cross their minds: *It must be hard to live with him,* and *How awful to be confined to a wheelchair.* They judge the quality of our lives without even knowing us.

People don't know that those skinny arms are actually very strong. Bret likes to arm wrestle, his big hands and slender fingers engulfing my hand as he drives it down. Sometimes he beats me, which he loves. Those legs that never seem to move have a story of their own. He has had operations to attach his legs to his hips with screws. He also has had his hamstrings surgically lengthened. That slurred jumble of words that seems to make no sense is sometimes a joke, and always very funny. "Go cry me a river" is his favorite wisecrack. His back has been twisted by scoliosis and eighteen years of muscle spasticity; it's so badly curved that his spine can be felt through his stomach.

This spine curvature hurts, too. Even though he rarely says anything, I can tell. He will need more surgery soon. "I want to do it over vacation so I don't miss any of your basketball games or my hockey practices," he told me. Although I worry about Bret's next operation, I know he doesn't because that's how he is. He always thinks of his family first.

People have no idea what it's like to live with a handicapped brother. Sure, it's hard sometimes, but I wouldn't trade it for the world. I wouldn't want to miss out on all the awesome things a person like Bret has to offer. I know there are limitations to what people in a wheelchair can do, but because of Bret, I also know their potential.

Last year, while cheering me on at one of my volleyball games, Bret declared out of the blue, "Mom, I wanna do something where I can get a medal. I wanna be on a team and win." Now, he is part of an adaptive floor-hockey team. His team placed third at the state tournament, and I have never seen him happier. When they placed that white ribbon with a shiny bronze medal around his neck he just beamed! His smile lasted for days . . . the same smile he wore when he bowled a 268 in his bowling league.

Bret is neither a burden nor an inconvenience; he's a blessing to my whole family. Anyone who gets to know him beyond "the kid in a wheelchair" will be impressed by what he has achieved. I have no idea what his limits are, but for now, I will always be by his side. I will be there to guide him, to cheer him on, and to be his teacher. The best thing is, I know he will always be there for me, too.

So, don't be quick to judge a person who seems different from you. My brother Bret has taught me there is much more to a person than meets the eye.

Mallory Dzubay

Reprinted by permission of Mike Shapiro. ©2007 Mike Shapiro.

Race Matters

*P*rejudice is the burden that confuses the past,
threatens the future, and renders the present
inaccessible.

Maya Angelou

I am a black woman, and for the longest time, I
was racist.

Love has overwhelmed me, as well as deep sadness,
because of someone whom I never thought I would meet.
When he came into my life, he altered the way I think, feel,
and live. Now I know what it means when one human can
have a lasting effect on another. Just one moment can
change you forever. I learned to feel. I learned to love. I
learned to see things for what they really are. And I
learned to forgive those who do not see. The man who
changed me happened to be white.

My past and present had told me that loving a white
man was not the same as loving a black soul brother.
When I think about that now, a slight laugh arises. Time
had told me interracial relationships were unethical,

disgraceful, and unsuccessful.

Love can have a powerful effect on people, but so can hatred. Both are aggressive. Both are stubborn. Some say that hate cannot destroy love, but if you had seen what I had, your outlook would be shattered. Tears form in my eyes because hate is destroying my love for him—a love that I didn't plan, a love I didn't want.

Society told me I couldn't love him. Society told me I shouldn't love him. Society told me this, and society told me that. My ears had been cemented with these words, and so I tried to convince myself that I couldn't love him. Those words filled my mouth, but then I realized the words were theirs and not mine. I had none of my own. I had to create my own. The combination of my love and their hate drove me to perceive that my society did not know about color blindness.

I have been subjected to old-fashioned racism—black people are like this; white people are like that. People fighting because they dislike the other's skin tone, and reverse racism where my own people hated me for being with this man, this white man I love dearly.

My mind was manipulated by society from the day I was born, but this awareness dawned slowly. It demolished my foundation, and then it pushed me to think. *How can something like love destroy a foundation that is supposed to be solid? How can it be destroyed unless it wasn't strong to begin with?*

Now, I see nothing but a radiant light in my mind. I have assembled a new foundation, even though at first I hated myself for loving him. The person I was before is a person I regret being. I was ignorant.

I've learned two important things. First, love itself is timeless, colorless, and honest. But the most important lesson that will be branded on my mind forever is that race *does* matter.

Being a certain race is not just the color of your skin; it's who you are, where you live, and how you live. It's the situations you live, the decisions you make, and their consequences. It's what blood you're born from. It's your teachings. It's what you stand for. It's everything your ancestors were and believed in. The past and the color of your skin are what makes you *you*. You can either embrace diversity with pure love, or resist it with pure hatred, but in either case, race does matter. But then again, it doesn't.

My racism might have destroyed a love I didn't even know I wanted. The reality of something pure has disrupted my existence. It doesn't matter what I was, because I don't see that anymore. All I see and all I know is this moment, this pen and this paper, this hand and this mind. Love has given me something I didn't even think that I needed—realization.

Now I kneel on a concrete foundation, looking out into an empty, endless space, and I'm terrified that the person I was before will not allow the person I am now to stand.

Marquise Jones

9

MONUMENTAL MOMENTS

The future belongs to those who believe in the beauty of their dreams.

Eleanor Roosevelt

Who Am I?

You can't turn back the clock. But you can wind it up again.

Bonnie Prudden

I am seventeen years young, not even an adult yet. I cannot buy cigarettes or vote. I have only been driving for a year and a half. I have completed only twelve years of school. It will be four years until I can legally drink an alcoholic beverage. I am only seventeen years young, and yet I have seen and experienced so much. So much, that it makes the future seem boring.

I have tasted the bad. I have broken hearts. I have broken the law. I have kissed boys. I have kissed girls. I have played with fire. I have lied and cheated and stolen, and I have been caught. I have gone over the speed limit. I have skipped church. I have created mischief. I have binged and purged. I have made people cry. I have made mistakes.

I have tasted the ugly. I have had my heart broken. I have witnessed close friends come out. I have witnessed closer friends struggle with self-mutilation. I have had fights with my best friends for petty reasons. I have created drama as well as participated in it. I have had panic attacks and social anxiety and been the victim of mild depression. I have used the words "I hate you" too many times.

I have witnessed and tasted the good, the bad, and the ugly in just seventeen years. I regret countless things I have said and done. I am rotten to my core for all the horrible details of my seventeen years of life.

But . . . this is not what matters.

What matters is the good. What matters are the times I have listened, the times I have offered my shoulder to a sobbing friend. What matters is the difference I made in someone's life, whether helping with homework, sharing a smile, or calling just to say hello. What matters is the hard work I do and the recognition I receive. What matters is the memories I have made, the laughs I have shared, and the bonds I have kept. What matters is the strong and unique individual I have become. What matters is the exemplary, mature woman I have become by learning from my mistakes when I was still an ignorant, little girl in the past seventeen years of my life. All that matters is the good.

Mary Buehler

Life in the Middle Lane

Life is 10 percent what you make it and 90 percent how you take it.

Irving Berlin

Have you ever noticed how frequently and how easily cars switch lanes on the highway? If the car in front of you is moving too slowly, you simply move to a faster lane. Sure, fluctuating between the dotted lines too often is not the most intelligent plan, but it can be quite an adrenaline rush. While some have their own personal lanes—the old ladies and cautious drivers restrict their safety zone to the slow lane, while those with inflated egos and a need for speed hurtle down the fast lane—the sacred middle lane is reserved for those in between.

Webster's Dictionary defines adolescence as the time of life between puberty and maturity. If I were Webster, I would change the definition slightly. Being a teenager today is not so much a time of life as it is a series of moments strung together with a little uncertainty and a lot of stress; it is primarily a time of significance. I like to refer to us as "in-betweeners" because we could not possibly be more stuck in the middle of life if we tried. Since I am sixteen, not only am I caught in the middle of society, but I am also caught in the middle of being a teenager—right between thirteen and nineteen.

No longer do my days consist of sand castles and Play-Doh, recess and snack time. Barney and Big Bird are friends of the past, as are Barbie and hopscotch. Yet, at the other end of the spectrum, I still cannot vote, I still live with my parents, and I still have no idea how cruel the "real world" really is. I am torn between the desire to rekindle the joys of childhood and the need to keep maturing and become an adult. I want to be more, and at the same time, I want to be less. I want to go back to a time when life was simpler and made more sense, but I want to be independent and find my own way. I am no longer a child, yet not an adult.

But what is being a teenager, really? A constant headache or a pimple that shows up the night of a date? A time of insecurities and peer pressure? An excuse for parties and testing just how much we can get away with? I think not. I think being a teenager is a midpoint, signifying a step away from the comforts of home, but with a foot in the doorway for security's sake. Sure, we may not hold great political power, have discovered the cure for cancer, or found out why or how or who, but give us some time. We are the future. No matter how hard our parents and teachers and elders may try, they will never be able to reclaim their past. At least we have one thing they do not. But, seriously, if we put life into perspective, what greater time is there than adolescence?

If we think back to our childhood, we may think that life used to be perfect and that we would give anything to be a kid again. But what fun would regressing to that be, knowing what we know now? (And, believe me, teenagers hear things, see things, and know more than adults give us credit for.) For how long would Play-Doh and building blocks hold our attention? And would we really be satisfied being told what to do and never having the chance to know why things are done a certain way or the knowledge to change things? On the other hand, are we ready for a mortgage and car payments? Are we prepared to get married and raise a family and give all of ourselves to another? Can we even imagine giving up the freedom and irresponsibility that is allowed with adolescence for the stress that our parents endure?

Think for a minute. The very wise Dr. Seuss said, "Oh, the places you'll go . . ." and it's true. The places we will go will be exciting and new and challenge us in every way imaginable. And the places we have been will provide us with a foundation. All the hardships and insecurities we endured as teenagers will prepare us for the world, combined with our knowledge of how to have fun and live a simple life.

So, we see, adolescence is such an important stage that it should be embraced, not shunned. Respected and not questioned. Enjoyed and not rushed. It is not yet life in the fast lane, but it is a graduation from the slow lane, where new drivers and old ladies drive under the speed limit because they are too scared to test the waters. Adolescence is full of ups and downs, good and bad, struggle and strife, rewards and accomplishments. In a word, it is full.

So for all the teenagers out there, if you ever feel like you cannot handle adolescence anymore, remember how great life in the middle lane can be, and just cruise.

Sara Cafarelli

The Making of a Man

It was the beginning of gym class, and I set down my belongings in the most secluded area of the boys' locker room. I felt my simple, undeveloped body was inferior to the libido-loaded adolescents who ruled the locker room, and I wanted to avoid confrontation with them. My worst fear had always been that someone was going to sneak up and pilfer my undergarments, which would then force me to chase after this B.V.D. bandit in my birthday suit.

I was stripping off my clothes in the process of changing into my uniform, when the incandescence of a single chest hair caught my eye. I paused for a moment and looked down at God's gift. There it was: dark, silky, and beautiful, the only one of its kind. And I thought to myself, *After one, more are sure to follow.*

I was at that age when boys suddenly change from boys to, well, not men, but something in between the two— demented, terrifying creatures known as adolescents. By the time I entered this stage, most of my friends were well underway in their journey toward manhood. All around me droned the chorus of squeaky, semi-low-pitched male voices, and I, with my soprano voice, came to the realization that I, too, would be dragged to the same fate as the others. I was, however, what is considered a "late bloomer" and, unlike my classmates, had not yet developed.

A few months after my chest-hair sighting, my voice began its gradual and cruel change. Whenever I spoke, an embarrassing, indescribable chirp would escape from my mouth. Usually, I could not even speak a full sentence without my voice jumping an octave or two. But I realized that all us guys go through this, so I could deal with it.

The last drastic change from boy to adolescent was libido control. Because I was late in blooming, I had witnessed the drastic effects libido had on other males. No longer were the boys happy with each other's company. They were in search of something else: the sexual unknown. The devil of puberty turns every young male into an uncontrollable mass of hormones whose every waking moment is occupied by the thought of the female gender.

I, too, succumbed to the natural fascination with women, but in a different way. Once I developed an interest, I, like many others, wanted a girlfriend—but I was certainly unprepared for the role of being a boyfriend. I remember the tumultuous experience of my first girlfriend. At the end of English class, all corners of the room were filled with the drone of students packing up to hurry to their next period. I was leaning over my belongings in a state of confusion when I felt something grab at my behind. To my surprise, my future girlfriend was standing behind me with the look of a criminal who had just gotten away with murder. My face turned a deep tint of scarlet as I searched the room for a witness to her crime. Luckily, nobody had noticed.

I attempted to say something, but all that came out of my mouth was a stutter. Feeling embarrassed, I ran for the exit, books and papers all jumbled in my arms. My only thought was to escape from the room and find a secluded stall in the men's bathroom to see if she had inflicted any superficial damage. Whenever anyone touched me, I had the habit of checking for an out-of-place ruffle in my clothes, but thankfully, I was unscathed.

Later that month, I somehow got dragged into a relationship with that same girl. The night I went to meet her mom and dad was another incident I will never forget. I was in their guest bathroom combing my hair, since I was about to meet her parents, and I wanted to look presentable. Out of the corner of my eye, I saw the door creep open and my girlfriend enter. "What are you . . ." my voice jumped an octave, "doing?"

"Oh, nothing," she replied, with the same look on her face she had had the day she accosted me in English class. For weeks, she had hinted that she wanted to engage in the ritual of kissing, even though I was completely terrified of her intentions. At that moment, I felt like a lost mouse being stalked by a great owl.

I had never been alone in a bathroom with a girl before, and I had no idea how to go about kissing. I had read many magazines on the topic, but they were no help. I was worried that my inexperience would cause me to falter. I wondered, as she edged closer and closer, when our lips come together, then what? My heart began to beat faster and faster. I looked around for a way out, but she had me cornered. I let out the loudest scream I could humanly produce and then jumped under her legs in an attempt to escape. Crawling the length of the bathroom, I scrambled to the exit as quickly as I could. My way was blocked by four knees, two covered with pants and two bulging out from the top of red-and-green argyle knee socks. I looked up to see her parents staring down at me.

"Hi!" again my voice cracked. "I'm Rob," I said while offering them my trembling, sweaty hand. They received it politely and asked if everything was okay. The door opened behind me, and my girlfriend exited. "Hi, Mom, Dad," she said as she blithely walked around the corner and disappeared from view.

Looking back, I learned that behind every cracking voice, sweaty palm, and sexually accosted boy, there is a mature, honest, responsible man in the making. The memory of the lone chest-hair sighting that I so gleefully discovered in the locker room is a savored memory tucked away with the squeeze on the behind and my first kiss. Maybe adolescence was not so bad after all.

Rob Dangel

"Didn't you have a crewcut the last time I looked up?"

Titration

Haven't you ever wanted
to distill yourself?
To take a part of you and
do like you did in high-school chemistry?
Boil away the iniquities, the insecurities,
the pettiness, and spitefulness,
evaporate the hatred, and then
To take what's left,
the quintessential salt that will not be cast out,
and cast it over the ones you love, saying,
"This is who I am."

Scott Molony

The Pond

They won't last long, school days and childish things,
We're moving up, going our separate ways.
Enjoy your future, all the changes and shifts.
And remember these years were precious gifts.

Maria Lamlin

My life is young. There is a certain purity to it, like new-fallen snow. I am teetering between being a child and being a woman. Each day I balance carefully, trying to reconcile the girl with the emerging adult.

There was a night, however, when this balancing act fell away, and youth was exactly where I wanted to be. It was the weekend of my seventeenth birthday, a Saturday, and the May air was warm, steeped in the smell of damp earth and sunshine. My friend Haley was hosting dinner, and we lounged on her patio, talking and laughing. I was giddy from too much ice cream and lovely birthday gifts.

We danced to every kind of music, spinning around Haley's living room and laughing until it hurt. Allisa, Gabi, James, and the others, all my dearest friends, were linked by a gossamer thread and an unbreakable bond. When the dancing ended, I lay on the carpet, dizzy from twirling, in a state of bliss. It was a feeling I had forgotten—one that surged from a place deep within me and sparkled in the open air.

As the sun dipped low, turning the clouds pink, our revelry quieted, and a content calm set in. We wandered down to the edge of Haley's pond, a small oasis bordered by willow trees and the cheerful croaking of frogs. The soft lamplight of the neighbors' windows was barely visible through the trees.

"I wish we could swim here," I said longingly, watching a dainty ripple work its way to the center.

"I have an idea," someone said, "for the birthday girl." When the plan was explained, we all agreed, though Haley glanced reluctantly toward her house.

"I hope my parents won't mind," she murmured. But it was too late for second thoughts. Gabi and the boys had been sent to fetch what we needed to create our masterpiece. The pond would be our canvas.

As we waited by the water, I climbed into the low boughs of the willow tree and dangled my legs over, letting my sandals slide off with a quiet thunk in the dark. Soon, the envoy returned with boxes of floating candles. Gabi led them down to the water, her long hair swinging.

We gathered, and I felt a small twinge in my side, of excitement, maybe, or goodness. Nothing was amiss in the world tonight.

Gabi lit the first candle carefully, reverently, and handed it to me.

"Happy birthday," she said warmly. I knelt at the water's edge. Smooth rocks pressed the bottoms of my feet. Everyone grew quiet and watched as I set the candle on the water. The small flame flickered but kept burning, casting a fragile shadow on the bottom of the pond. We watched it for a moment, and I was transported. It seemed like something I had read in a book once upon a time. I began to think the only thing that mattered was this solitary candle on the pond. The troubles of our adolescence lifted, and I knew what it was to be perfectly happy.

I turned back to the others. Wrapped in a quilt, Allisa was sitting peacefully where the grass met the pond. She gave me a smile, and I saw her eyes dancing with the brightening light of the moon. Gabi was lighting the next candle, her face framed in a halo of soft light. She handed this one to James, who set it next to mine. We worked silently, sending dozens of candles into the night. They illuminated the air around them. Someone hummed softly. Haley kept watch, lest the night be spoiled by the arrival of a grown-up.

There was only a slight breeze, and the candles stayed close to shore.

"I'm wading in," I said, intrigued by the glow of the water. It looked like tea and honey out in the middle.

"I'll go, too," said James. We rolled up our cuffs and started in, careful not to tip the candles. The sand was soft. I felt myself sinking a little, and I grabbed his hand. The water lapped softly at my ankles as we waded toward the center. I moved my toes, creating a tiny current, urging the candles to float farther. The more we moved, the deeper I sank into the mud, and soon my jeans were soaked past the knees. At one point, the silty bottom gave way, and I lost my balance. James caught me, and we both started laughing, though I felt a strange urge to stifle it.

The night was like a sanctuary, worshipful and still. *Nutrimentum spiritus,* I heard in the wind. Food for the soul. There was a soulful quality, of friendship and deep connection. For a fleeting second, I had the notion that the glow of the pond was not from the candles, but from us.

Eventually we left the pond and settled on the grass, heads together, talking softly. The stars were bright.

Jennifer Phelps

Polly Want a Cracker?

I have never let my schooling interfere with my education.

Mark Twain

It is true . . . I am, or should I say was, a parrot. Yes, un-knowingly, when I was a child, I became a parrot. I do not know the exact date, but it occurred during my elementary school years. And I was one of the best parrots in the school. How did I become one? Well, because of school.

Between the ages of seven and ten, I sprouted my first set of feathers. This was probably because there were no more toys in the classroom, and we had only a half-hour of playtime during the six-hour day. This made school boring. I wanted to be done as quickly as possible. The teachers did not care, and the classes were so large that no one got individual attention. The teachers had to make up tests that were a little challenging, but easy enough so everyone could pass. I was ahead of the rest of the class. When the test came, I knew I would get a good mark if I just knew the gist of what we were studying. In most of my classes, the test came right from the homework or notes, so why think? All I had to do was memorize. My beak developed in junior high, when thinking was definitely not necessary. My book reports were simply summaries with nothing added. I remember one time the entire class handed in ten-page reports. The next morning they were returned with a letter grade and few comments.

The whistle after I speak developed shortly after my beak. This is when the parrot really shows his colors. One time in science class, we were taking notes. I went to the bathroom, and the teacher corrected some information he had given us. When I returned, no one told me. For the test, I answered a question exactly as I had "learned" in my notes, not realizing that the answer was contradictory and made no sense. So, of course, I got it wrong and failed. Still not realizing my condition, I went back to eating my crackers and honey nuggets.

I was a full parrot upon entering high school. And there, I learned how to fly. That made me realize I was stuck in a cage, but not until sophomore year when I took the PSAT. I scored an 1130. Now, this is not bad, but I had had a 98 average all my life, and an 1130 just didn't match. It was my chance to shine, and I did not. Rather, I could not, because that was the best I could do.

So even though my brain could fly, I was trapped in a little educational cage I had made for myself by taking the easy way out in school. Now I had to unlearn what I had been doing for my school career. I had to open the cage.

I started molting the middle of sophomore year. At first I did it manually, plucking off each feather of laziness and procrastination. Once those feathers were gone, the rest fell out naturally. Surprisingly, the process was not hard. That summer I picked up my first book to read for pleasure, *X-Men* by Diane Duani. As soon as I opened it, my love for reading began. In junior year, all my feathers had fallen out, and I had started going back to what I was meant to be . . . a human being with a fully functional brain.

But then I realized something: some of my classes required me to be a parrot. That was the only way I could pass. The teachers just wanted to hear what they told us in their lectures. I complied but also learned the material so that I could use it to open the cage. I listened to the advice of Mark Twain: "Never let schooling interfere with your education."

Dominick Vargas

Reflection in the Skies

Most children's first words range from primal grunts to sweet mumblings that resemble human names, but my first word was "thunder." From the very beginning, I have been captivated with the sky and its ever-changing canvas of blues and grays, creams and milky whites. I am tuned in to the rhythms of rainfall, the dance of snowflakes, and the flutter of clouds across the sky. One can always find me gazing out my window, hoping that the storms most people dread actually come my way. I remember setting up my own storm-viewing station in the garage the year Connecticut was in the direct path of Hurricane Bob. The weather channel became *my* program, and I was a third-grader mesmerized by weather forecasts and terminology. A few years later, in the middle of a blizzard, I remember running wildly up the stairs to tell my parents we were in an "upper level low." Since then, both my vocabulary and interest have matured, but I still have my dog-eared cloud chart by my bed.

After so many years of standing guard at the window, straining to hear the low roars crawl through the sky, I am struck by the many ways I am a thunderstorm. Contrary to what this may seem like, I am neither volatile nor explosive. Rather, I am a presence that others can sense, always ready to contribute my thoughts. I am told I have a passion for living because I am always the one who laughs the hardest and enjoys each moment. I am exceedingly strong-willed and independent, not afraid to express opinions or open my heart. I feel most alive when engaged in conversations that require persuasion, and most powerful when others challenge me. And, while I fight to support my beliefs with the ferocity of an unrelenting storm, my winds of dissent quell easily when I encounter clear and reasoned counterpoints. I entered high school an average student but am leaving a serious scholar.

While thunder and I are alike in many ways, we have our differences, too. Thunder tends to strike suddenly with bombastic blasts, then dissipate and stop as abruptly as it began. In contrast, I am not unpredictable, or a burst of energy followed by a complete silence. My path is fixed, and I am steady as I move along my charted course. As I advance, there is an unmistakable pattern to my movements, based on my unyielding desire to question and to know.

Thunder has also taught me lessons about life and has had a humbling impact on me. Its loud blasts are powerful announcements that suggest the vulnerability of humankind and the existence of a greater force. With every passing storm, I am reminded that God is a guiding energy, stronger than any earthly conflict. I look ahead with confidence because of his presence and my will to soar.

Just as the clouds begin their elegant sweep across the sky, the leaves quiver as if they have felt a chill, and the scent of rain sweetens the air, I, too, am just beginning. When I look at clouds overhead, I see them filled with opportunity and a rain that can only help to make me grow.

Allison Briggs

"Let me guess: I shouldn't be afraid
to follow my dream, right?"

Princesses

I believe in looking reality straight in the eye and denying it.

Garrison Keillor

Don't deny it; every little girl is a princess. At sleep-overs, we did each other's makeup. Looking back, I know that the moms who said we looked pretty were being wonderfully merciful. But we were princesses, and we were beautiful, and every girl was special, unique, and kind. We were never as mean as we are now because, in the end, we remembered our royal roots and that we were princesses. Every little girl dreamed that the boy she liked would do something heroic or dashing like in Disney movies.

That's the part we all know. What I want to know now is, when does the princess realize she is going to have to get out of the castle on her own? I'm only fifteen, but already the girls in my class have torn dresses and disheveled tiaras because we're escaping the dragon-guarded castle. When do the girls stop thinking there is a prince? Is it when they really get to know a boy?

I stopped being a princess long ago when I realized there is a reason fairy tales are so enticing: nobody's life is a fairy tale, no matter how good it may seem. It's funny. I'll think someone in school has it all and feel envious. She never threw away her tiara, I'll think, passing her in the hall with her knight. Then, when I get to know her, she will tell me things that stain the pages I had created for her, and another life I thought was a fairy tale isn't.

In a way, every girl I know is more into theatrics than they realize. When I was mad at my boyfriend and somebody asked if everything was okay, I just nodded, because we have lost the tiaras down one of those dark corridors, the glass slippers are long gone (maybe in a box in the attic), and that Halloween costume we wore doesn't fit anymore. We want to believe, and subconsciously we would also like others to.

We want people to think our life is a fairy tale, even though we know it isn't. There are girls who are always crying over everything; they want people to think their life is exciting and dramatic. People like me, who never have any excitement, are envious that they have so much. Maybe that's why the girl who is no longer with the boy still waves at him, although later, she wonders why. It's because of the fairy tale.

Don't the prince and princess always get back together? If we can convince each other that our lives are fairy tales like we played when we were princesses, maybe we can convince ourselves, too. That's not far from the truth, that feeling we get when something that seems "too good to be true" happens . . . that's when we can almost believe, and it is just like old times when we did each other's makeup at sleepovers, back when we were princesses.

Ashley Strickler

Raspberries

Brittle bushes thrash my young skin.
Thorns prickle the cuticles on my right fingers.
I hold in my left hand a tiny basket
filled with raspberries.
My father
helps me
escape the bushes,
a forest only as tall as his arms, and my mother
puts those ruby berries in a place
not even my longest finger
could reach:
the top of the refrigerator.
My lips smacked shut, closed out my tongue
from serenading the last berry.
When my father enters,
his hands are dirty from the outside,
and with those dirty hands he picks me up, and
carries me to the white sink so we both wash
earth from our juice-smelling hands.
I kick off my shoes and always find a thorn
stuck to my sweaty white sock,
never understanding how it got there.

My mother pulls it out, always saying
that she warned me to watch where I was walking.
Now crystal tap water cleans the raspberries.
My teeth squeeze the tip of one,
and juice splatters onto my chin, not needing a napkin;
my tongue cleans the spot.
I have to eat this berry,
biting into its concave center
and slowly disposing of it down my throat,
    asking for more.
And more,
until there are no more.
I ate them all.
No more,
Not until next year.

Adam Kirshner

The Manual

One does not discover new lands without consenting to lose sight of the shore for a very long time.

André Gide

When I was born, I was presented with a single, glossy piece of paper. In the light reflecting from the paper, I found a stability to which I eagerly clung. It told me my name, gender, ethnicity, address, creed, and the amount in my parents' bank account. At the bottom, it warned, "Please do not lose this! These things will define you."

And surely they would.

I did not know why I should memorize these facts, but I did; there wasn't much to remember. The day I went to preschool, ten more glossy pages were added. It was more complicated than I thought. I learned that I should not wear blue, green, or black—these were boy colors. My mom hadn't known this, so I had to teach her. I guess she had forgotten that page of her manual. My favorite color had to be a girl color and should probably be pink for good measure. I was again reminded not to lose the papers. The

only problem was that I really liked blue, but I would sac-
rifice it.

If I thought I knew anything in preschool, it was nothing compared to what I learned in elementary school.
Here, twenty-five pages were handed to me. There were
heaps of rules to explain what types of friends I should
have, the stores where I must shop, and the activities I
must pursue. I was a dancer, thus, I should not be an athlete; I was smart, thus, I should read a lot.

Middle school was the largest stack yet. It was sixty-five
pages filled with complex formulas for popularity, dis-
cussing weight, and a stringent dress code. There were
bus rules and sleepover rules. The hardest lesson by far
was the rules for visiting the bathroom. Girls had to travel
in even-numbered groups, and while there at least three
minutes had to be spent talking about some friend who
hadn't come with us. "Do not stand out. Stick with your
friends." Again I followed the rules, but they were creating
problems. I didn't really see the point in strategic herding
to the bathroom. I couldn't stand the petty fights that all
these rules created. And I hated sleepovers!

By the beginning of high school, I had an even 100
pages. These conventions were set in stone, but the comfort that my cherished manual had always given me was
deteriorating. Now I was supposed to live by these rules.
I was supposed to value them, but I found they were making me miserable.

Then one last sheet of paper came to me. It arrived not
as the others had and was not glossy or white. This paper
was bent on the edges, and the text was a little smudged.
"Why do you care about these rules? Life gave you no
manual. Don't you know your own handwriting, stupid?"

I looked at that paper and compared it to the pristine,
hundred-page manual. My manual was self-imposed.

It was not a rapid or easy change to accept that the

petty things I valued as a child could be altered. I chucked the manual and started over, feeling as if a new lung had opened within my chest. It would be hard to create myself without rules, but if I could create new rules, I could also break them. The possibilities for the future are endless if you keep from limiting yourself.

Besides, I rather like the color blue.

Jacqueline Miraglia

More Chicken Soup?

Many of the stories and poems you have read in this book were submitted by readers like you who had read earlier Teen Ink and Chicken Soup for the Soul books. We publish many Chicken Soup for the Soul books every year. We invite you to contribute a story to one of these future volumes.

Stories may be up to twelve hundred words and must uplift or inspire. You may submit an original piece, something you have read, or your favorite quotation on your refrigerator door.

To obtain a copy of our submission guidelines and a listing of upcoming Chicken Soup books, please write, fax, or check one of our websites.

Please send your submissions to:

Chicken Soup for the Soul
website: www.chickensoup.com
P.O. Box 30880
Santa Barbara, CA 93130
fax: 805-563-2945

We will be sure that both you and the author are credited for your submission.

For information about speaking engagements, other books, audiotapes, workshops, and training programs, please contact any of our authors directly.

Supporting Others

In the spirit of supporting others, the publisher and coauthors of *Chicken Soup for the Teen Soul: Real Stories by Real Teens* will donate a portion of the proceeds of this book to the *Teen Ink*'s foundation.

Established in 1989, *Teen Ink* is a monthly magazine, website, and book series written entirely by teens for teens. The magazine has been embraced by schools and teenagers nationwide; more than three and a half million students read *Teen Ink* magazine every year.

Teen Ink empowers teenagers by publishing their words and works. It is dedicated to improving their reading, writing, and critical-thinking skills, while encouraging creativity and building self-esteem. After reading more than four hundred thousand submissions from students over the past eighteen years, the editors have selected more than thirty-five thousand pieces for publication. There is no charge to submit work, and all published students receive a free copy of the magazine plus other items.

In keeping with its mission, the *Teen Ink*'s foundation distributes thousands of class sets and individual copies of *Teen Ink* magazine free to schools and teachers every month. In addition, more than twenty-four hundred schools support the foundation by paying a subsidized fee for their monthly class sets.

From its beginnings as a regional publication, *Teen Ink* has grown steadily and today is a national program funded by donations, sponsorships, private grants, and advertising from companies that support its goals. In addition to funding the magazine, the foundation uses grants and donations to underwrite the following programs:

The *Teen Ink* website (www.TeenInk.com) includes the magazine and many other interactive features and services with eighteen thousand pages of fiction, nonfiction, poetry, book, movie and music reviews, art, photos, and more. This website is the largest of its kind on the Internet with millions of visitors every year. Twenty thousand teenagers use TeenInk.com to submit their works directly to the magazine.

Teen Ink Poetry Journal showcases more than one thousand teenage poets and is distributed free to subscribing schools three times a year.

Teen Ink Educator of the Year Awards Contest welcomes nominating essays from students to honor outstanding teachers with cash prizes and publication of student essays in the magazine.

Teen Ink Book Awards donates thousands of free books and award materials so schools can recognize students who have shown "improvement and individual growth in the field of English."

Teen Ink Interview Contest encourages thousands of teens to interview family and friends, with the winners interviewing national celebrities, such as First Lady Barbara Bush, Sen. Hillary Clinton, Gen. Colin Powell, Sen. John Glenn, Rev. Jesse Jackson, Caroline Kennedy, Sir James and Lady Jeanne Galway, Maya Angelou, George Lucas, Ice Cube, Pedro Martinez, and Alicia Keys.

Who Is Jack Canfield?

Jack Canfield is the cocreator and editor of the Chicken Soup for the Soul series, which *Time* magazine has called "the publishing phenomenon of the decade." The series includes more than 140 titles with over 100 million copies in print in forty-seven languages. Jack is also the coauthor of eight other bestselling books, including *The Success Principles™: How to Get from Where You Are to Where You Want to Be, Dare to Win, The Aladdin Factor, You've Got to Read This Book,* and *The Power of Focus: How to Hit Your Business, Personal and Financial Targets with Absolute Certainty.*

Jack has recently developed a telephone coaching program and an online coaching program based on his most recent book, *The Success Principles.* He also offers a seven-day Breakthrough to Success seminar every summer, which attracts 400 people from about fifteen countries around the world.

Jack is the CEO of Chicken Soup for the Soul Enterprises and the Canfield Training Group in Santa Barbara, California, and is founder of the Foundation for Self-Esteem in Culver City, California. He has conducted intensive personal and professional development seminars on the principles of success for more than a million people in twenty-nine countries around the world. Jack is a dynamic keynote speaker, and he has spoken to hundreds of thousands of others at more than 1,000 corporations, universities, professional conferences, and conventions and has been seen by millions more on national television shows such as *Oprah, Montel, The Today Show, Larry King Live, Fox and Friends, Inside Edition, Hard Copy, CNN's Talk Back Live, 20/20, Eye to Eye,* and the *NBC Nightly News* and the *CBS Evening News.* Jack was also a featured teacher in the hit movie *The Secret.*

Jack is the recipient of many awards and honors, including three honorary doctorates and a Guinness World Records Certificate for having seven books from the Chicken Soup for the Soul series appearing on the *New York Times* bestseller list on May 24, 1998.

To write to Jack or for inquiries about Jack as a speaker, his coaching programs, trainings, or seminars, use the following contact information:

Jack Canfield
The Canfield Companies
P.O. Box 30880 • Santa Barbara, CA 93130
phone: 805-563-2935 • fax: 805-563-2945
E-mail: info4jack@jackcanfield.com
www.jackcanfield.com

Who Is Mark Victor Hansen?

In the area of human potential, no one is more respected than Mark Victor Hansen. For more than thirty years, Mark has focused solely on helping people from all walks of life reshape their personal vision of what's possible. His powerful messages of possibility, opportunity, and action have created powerful change in thousands of organizations and millions of individuals worldwide.

He is a sought-after keynote speaker, bestselling author, and marketing maven. Mark's credentials include a lifetime of entrepreneurial success and an extensive academic background. He is a prolific writer with many bestselling books, such as *The One Minute Millionaire, Cracking the Millionaire Code, How to Make the Rest of Your Life the Best of Your Life, The Power of Focus, The Aladdin Factor,* and *Dare to Win,* in addition to the Chicken Soup for the Soul series. Mark has made a profound influence through his library of audios, videos, and articles in the areas of big thinking, sales achievement, wealth building, publishing success, and personal and professional development.

Mark is the founder of the MEGA Seminar Series. MEGA Book Marketing University and Building Your MEGA Speaking Empire are annual conferences where Mark coaches and teaches new and aspiring authors, speakers, and experts on building lucrative publishing and speaking careers. Other MEGA events include MEGA Info-Marketing and My MEGA Life.

As a philanthropist and humanitarian, Mark works tirelessly for organizations such as Habitat for Humanity, American Red Cross, March of Dimes, Childhelp USA, and many others. He is the recipient of numerous awards that honor his entrepreneurial spirit, philanthropic heart, and business acumen. He is a lifetime member of the Horatio Alger Association of Distinguished Americans, an organization that honored Mark with the prestigious Horatio Alger Award for his extraordinary life achievements.

Mark Victor Hansen is an enthusiastic crusader of what's possible and is driven to make the world a better place.

Mark Victor Hansen & Associates, Inc.
P.O. Box 7665 • Newport Beach, CA 92658
phone: 949-764-2640 • fax: 949-722-6912
www.markvictorhansen.com

Who Are Stephanie and John Meyer?

Stephanie and John Meyer are the publishers of *Teen Ink* magazine and TeenInk.com (formerly known as *The 21st Century*), which they founded in 1989 when their own children were teenagers. The Meyers believed that teens should have the opportunity to share their ideas, concerns, and creativity with their peers in a larger forum than their high school. They also recognized that teens have a great deal to say and felt that it was important for their voices to be heard. After more than eighteen years, *Teen Ink* magazine has published forty-five thousand works, and the magazine is read by millions of teenagers nationwide and on the web through TeenInk.com.

Stephanie Meyer, senior editor of the *Teen Ink* book series and magazine, holds master's degrees in education and social work. She has always been an advocate for children and young people, first as a teacher and then as a social worker, as well as a mother and community activist. She has found much joy in reading and selecting the pieces for the magazine each month. Stephanie is also an avid reader, despite her daily dose of editorial work, as well as enjoying yoga, walking, and now her two grandsons.

John Meyer, with an M.B.A. from the Stern School at NYU, is the publisher of the magazine and president of the magazine's nonprofit foundation. Prior to *Teen Ink*, John was an insurance broker and risk manager for many corporations and then was the founder and publisher of two other publications, *Insurance Times* and *Financial Services Times*. John spends any free time he can jogging, making and editing videos, and traveling periodically with Stephanie.

After ten years, Stephanie and John became the compilers of the successful *Teen Ink* book series, culling through all the back issues to create a showcase for some of the strongest and most compelling pieces. Health Communications, Inc., published the six-book series over a three-year period. And now with the help of the Chicken Soup series, more of these teen works by teens of today and yesterday will be enjoyed by everyone.

Contributors

Maria Adelmann graduated from college with a double major in English and psychology and a concentration in creative writing. Her work has been published in national books and magazines. Maria has little idea what's coming next, but she hopes to find a creative job that involves writing, film, or craft projects.

Daniel Bailey received his bachelor of science with honors. He is currently pursuing a doctorate degree in theoretical physics. Daniel enjoys reading, writing, and listening to good music.

At the age of thirty-two, **Natascha Batchelor** became a professional arborist. As such, she is privileged to spend time visiting unique landscapes with breathtaking views of the Cape Cod shores. Her career defines her, and she dedicates her heart and soul to it.

Rebecca Bodfish earned her bachelor of arts and a law degree. Rebecca currently resides in Massachusetts, where she practices media and intellectual property law.

Emma Bodnar lives on Canada's west coast. She marvels at the natural world surrounding her and has a passion for expressing this wonder in her stories and poems. Some of her hobbies include reading, sports, and music.

Stacy Boudreau received her bachelor of science degree in developmental psychology. She hopes to work with people of all ages who have developmental disabilities. She also enjoys hiking, camping, kayaking, aerobics, reading, and music. Please e-mail her at Stacy2686@comcast.net.

Mariel Boyarsky is an undergraduate student, pursuing an independent major in gender studies and linguistics. She has always enjoyed writing, particularly nonfiction and poetry. In her spare time she enjoys reading, playing ultimate Frisbee, and hanging out with her dog, Cinderella. Please e-mail her at maboyarsky@vassar.edu.

Allison Briggs is currently a junior in college. Last semester she was given the privilege to venture out of the country to study in Florence, Italy. She plans on graduating in 2008 with a double major in elementary education and theological studies and pursuing a career as a primary educator.

Andrew G. Briggs received his bachelor of arts with honors. He presently works in human resources for a Fortune 100 company. Andrew is working toward his third pilot's license and plans to become a professional pilot. He also enjoys running, sports, being with friends, and continuing his passion for literature and writing. Please e-mail him at abriggs77@gmail.com.

Mary Buehler is currently studying communications in college and hopes to someday work in television or movies. She has written poems, essays, scripts, and plays and plans to continue writing in the future. For more of her work, contact her at mbuehler2@ithaca.edu.

Kimberly Burton is an electrical engineer and is pursuing her master's degree in engineering. She feels that political activism is important and was a founding board member of the Kansas Equality Coalition.

Sara Cafarelli is currently a junior studying public health and art history. She aspires to go to medical school and become a pediatrician. She loves traveling, skiing, working out, and spending time with her family.

Martha Campbell is a graduate of Washington University, St. Louis School of Fine Arts, and a former writer/designer for Hallmark cards. She has been a freelance cartoonist and book illustrator since 1973. She can be reached at P.O. Box 2538, Harrison, Arizona, or via e-mail at marthaf@alltel.net.

Emilee Castillo has been writing as a way to cope with her depression. A year following her hospitalization, she began a suicide-prevention program after her friend committed suicide. Emilee plans to help distressed teens by becoming a therapist. She hopes to publish more of her work in the near future.

Katherine Cincotta received her bachelor of arts and her master's in teaching of English. She is currently teaching ninth-grade English and an eighth-grade creative writing workshop class. Katherine continues to write and enjoys working with young writers while encouraging them to publish their work.

Helen Comber will graduate with a bachelor of science in music education in 2008. She hopes to enter a master's program in music therapy or teach middle school general/choral music. Helen and her family are thankful that Grandma Evelyn's memory is being shared with so many. Please send your favorite cookie recipes to hrc111@psu.edu!

Lyndsey Costello was in the seventh grade when she wrote "His Last Smile." She is now in eighth grade and is anticipating high school. Lyndsey loves hanging out with her best friend, talking on the phone, shopping, playing kickball, and reading.

Christina Courtemarche received a bachelor of arts in computer science. She works as a software engineer and enjoys hiking, solving puzzles, and reading. Please e-mail her at cjcourt@yahoo.com.

Rob Dangel received his bachelor of science in business. Rob is the father of three beautiful children. He looks forward to teaching them many life lessons learned every day. He enjoys computer gaming, movies, and spending time with his family. You can contact Rob at rdangel@gmail.com.

Nicole Docteur received her bachelor of arts in anthropology. She then received a master of library science. She is currently a secondary-school librarian.

Mallory Dzubay is currently studying kinesiology and plans on attending a two-year technical school for prosthetics after completing her undergraduate schooling. She is preparing for a career in the prosthetics field and cannot wait to help people like her brother.

Gulielma Fager received her master of public health. She is a writer, covering sexuality, sexual health, and health policy issues for a variety of publications. She also leads workshops on healthy sexuality for teens.

Angie Forest is a part-time administrative assistant and the mother of a three-year-old. She continues to enjoy writing and is still blessed with her Pepere in her life. She enjoys spending time with family, especially her son, and the outdoors.

Sharlyne Gan is currently a college student pursuing a nursing career. She began to express herself through writing in online diaries. A writer's workshop class in high school allowed her to find different forms of writing styles to best capture a moment. She continues to write through an online journal open to the public. Please e-mail her at heyyitzcharlie@hotmail.com.

AmyBeth Gardner writes several online blogs. She left a rewarding job in social work to pursue her lifelong dream of publishing a book of autobiographical poems, on which she continues to work. AmyBeth feels being a starving artist gives one a great deal of character.

Lisa Gauches studied music and theatre in college. She has worked in London, New York City, Connecticut, and California among other places. Lisa attributes what successes she has largely to luck, critical friends, a patient boyfriend, her parents' support, and her sibling's constant confusion on what she actually does for a living. She writes in her spare time.

Annie Gaughen received her master of arts in Scotland, where she is currently pursuing her master's in creative writing. An aspiring young-adult fiction novelist, she is translating her international travels into literary adventures. Please contact her at acgaughen@gmail.com.

David Gelbard entered college as a pitcher for the varsity baseball team and has maintained a 3.8 GPA in business administration. He was named Athlete of the Year by *Rockland Journal News* and has thirteen national publications. He founded the Gelbard Tutoring Company and interned at Citigroup the summer of 2006. He can be reached at dgelb11@aol.com.

Mai Goda received her bachelor of arts. She lives with her fiancé and their one-year-old pug in Connecticut.

Olivia Godbee is married and lives in Illinois. Olivia works full-time at a local bar and grill. Her hobbies include yoga, bicycling, fishing, and writing. Olivia plans to write a book of motivational and inspirational essays.

Micaela Golding received her bachelor of science in political science. In June 2007, she will earn a master's degree in national security affairs. Micaela is a surface warfare officer in the United States Navy. In her off-time, she enjoys reading, snowboarding, surfing, and watching professional sporting events.

In 2006, as a premed college student, **Valerie Gribben** founded Healing Words, an organization whose volunteers read books to hospital patients. *USA Today* chose Valerie for its 2007 All-USA College Academic First Team of students. Her *Fairytale Trilogy* will be published in 2008.

Yuliya (Julia) Gudish was born in Kiev, Ukraine, but hails from the suburbs of New York City. She is currently a freshman studying government, economics, and psychology. In addition to writing poetry, prose, and comedy monologues, Julia's passions include acting, competitive Latin ballroom dancing, belting jazz, sports, and dark chocolate.

Amanda Hager ponders ways to spend her days pursuing all her different dreams. She lives with her boyfriend, her Great Dane, Pablo, and her guinea pig, Elvis. E-mail her at karmasnow@hotmail.com.

Meghan Heckman is a staff writer for the *Concord (NH) Monitor* and has won numerous awards for her work as a journalist. She graduated from college and completed her fellowships at the Poytner Institute and the New York Times Foundation. She skies, knits, and runs marathons.

Holly Hester received her bachelor of arts in journalism. She is director of marketing for a firm in North Carolina. Holly enjoys travel, boating, tennis, hiking, art, wine, and music. She can be reached via e-mail at hhester@helenadamsrealty.com.

Anna Holmquist currently attends high school. She enjoys writing, reading, acting, learning Spanish, playing piano, and singing. Anna hopes to attend college and major in either Spanish or English. Please e-mail her at aeholmquist@yahoo.com.

Patti Hulett is majoring in secondary history and government education. Patti wrote "Stop! LEGO Thief!" in her tenth-grade English class taught by Mrs. Dawn Wilcox. Patti enjoys drinking coffee, watching *Grey's Anatomy*, and shopping for flip-flops.

Jason Jellies is studying biological sciences, chemistry, and the Russian language. He enjoyed writing as a student in high school and will enjoy reading until the day he dies or the day he goes blind, whichever comes first.

Ashley Johnston is leaving for the Air Force in July 2007. Ashley hopes to retire from the military twenty years from now. She loves the outdoors, especially horses and camping.

Marquise Jones attends college pursuing her bachelor's in political science. She enjoys writing, drawing, music, and politics. One day she hopes to create a new national political party and become president of the United States. Please e-mail her at mjones47@ucok.edu.

Steven Jones is currently studying language arts education. Steven writes for *The Oklahoma Daily* and plans to become a high-school journalism teacher or a sports journalist. His beard struggles continue to this day. You can e-mail Steven at steven.c.jones@tx.rr.com.

Lisa Kelly received her bachelor of science in journalism. In her spare time, she enjoys running, skiing, and spending time with her friends and family. She is also an avid fan of the New England Patriots and the Boston Red Sox. Lisa is grateful to the English department at her high school for introducing her to *Teen Ink* and allowing her to explore creative writing.

Courtney Kersten wrote "Room 103" as an eighth-grader in honor of her mother. Currently, Courtney studies theater. Among many fascinations, she passes time eavesdropping whenever possible and wandering through bookstores. Contact her at ck77@evansville.edu.

Olivia King is currently working as a registered nurse in a surgical ICU. She enjoys music, skiing, and spending time with her family and friends.

Adam Kirshner graduated from college with a business degree in marketing. He currently works in Connecticut as a television production assistant. For fun, Adam enjoys watching baseball, reading, watching movies, and, of course, writing. Adam hopes to one day incorporate his writings into episodic television.

Allyson Klein is a senior, earning a bachelor of arts in public relations communication and minoring in business leadership. Her active campus involvement includes: marketing/PR chair and webmaster for her sorority, as well as columnist/reporter for her school newspaper. Allyson enjoys traveling, working, dancing; spending time with her family, friends, and boyfriend; and the color pink.

Susan Landry received a bachelor of arts degree. She currently works as a successful freelance marketing copywriter and still enjoys writing fiction in her spare time. Susan lives with her husband, son, and two dogs in Rhode Island.

Kelly Jean Laubenheimer received her bachelor of science in business administration with honors. She currently works as a real estate agent in North Carolina where she resides with her husband,

Kevin, and their "pound puppy," Champ. To contact her, please e-mail kellyjvandeusen@yahoo.com.

Amy Hochsprung Lawton received her master of arts in teaching. She currently teaches English. She lives with her husband and young son. Outside the classroom, Amy spends most of her time hiking and exploring the great outdoors.

Kendra Lider-Johnson received her bachelor of arts and master of education. She wishes she still wrote as prolifically as she did in high school.

Jessica Lin received her bachelor of arts degree in English. She works as an educational researcher in New York City.

Kathleen McCarney's teen years were filled with angst and insecurity —except when she was writing in her journal. She still keeps a journal. While it continues to be for her eyes only, she now uses her skills in a small public relations firm.

Jacqueline Miraglia is pursuing an English/honors major with a French minor. She enjoys writing, dancing, and cooking. She has recently completed a children's chapter book called *Forks in the Fish Tank*. Jacqueline lives with her parents and brother.

Tiffany Mitchell received her bachelors in education degree. She has two daughters, ages one and six. Tiffany enjoys boating, camping, and motor sports with her family. She currently owns and operates her own child-care business, and she aspires to continue her education in the near future.

Scott Molony is beginning college in the fall. He plans to study philosophy and theology. Scott enjoys running, traveling, singing, and drinking tea. He is the team leader of the 2007 National Winners of the Siemens Competition in Math, Science, and Technology.

Kerri Morrone is the editor of *EXIST Magazine*, and creator and author of the award-winning diabetes blog, Six Until Me (www.sixuntilme.com). She works as an editor for dLife, a diabetes media company. Kerri is a health and fitness enthusiast, author, crackerjack Scrabble player, and quick to hit the beach. Drop her a line at kerri@sixuntilme.com.

Emily Newick received her bachelor of arts from Middlebury College and her master of public health. She works for a nonprofit organization providing eye care in the developing world.

George Newton teaches students how to express themselves in middle school.

Clara Nguyen is pursuing a bachelor of arts in art history. Clara loves art, books, and creativity. She plans on enjoying a career involving museum work.

Andrea Nickerson will graduate in the fall with a bachelor of science degree and a minor in elementary education. She enjoys traveling, teaching, being outdoors, and spending time with friends and family. After graduation she plans to move out of the Midwest and become a kindergarten teacher.

Amanda Caryn O'Loughlin received her bachelor's in fine arts and her master's in criminal justice. She is currently working in the field of public safety. Amanda is actively involved in AIDS education and has led Team Lodie in the annual AIDS Walk since the death of her uncle Joseph "Jay" Lodie in 1994. You may contact her at aoloughlin@comcast.net.

Jennifer Phelps attends a small liberal arts college in Minnesota and is pursuing bachelor of arts degrees in English and French. She grew up in Wisconsin and hopes someday to teach English or French literature at a university, and to continue writing.

Teresa Porter received her bachelor of arts in human services with honors. Teresa enjoys laughing with her new husband, traveling, and ministering at women's conferences. Please e-mail her at WriteOnTeresa@gmail.com.

Amie Barbone Powell wrote "A Forced Eruption" when she was in high school and obtained a bachelor of science in elementary education. Currently, she teaches first grade in the South. Amie and her husband are expecting their first child soon. Her hobbies include cooking, reading, spending time with her husband, and playing with their schnauzer, Zeke.

Kelly Powell received her bachelor of arts. She enjoys traveling, yoga, and spending time with her family. She plans to write inspirational children's books.

Dana Rusk is currently attending college and enjoys traveling, camping, and kayaking.

Sarah Miles Ryan is the second of five children. She graduated with honors and is currently a political science and history student. Upon graduation, she plans to move to New York City and pursue a career in journalism or education, specifically a job where she can engage in and hone her love of words.

Clair Saeger wrote her essay as a junior in high school. Today, Clair is a junior in college. She is a communication major who hopes this is the beginning of a long career. Clair continues to look at her family for inspiration and thanks them for all their life lessons. She can be reached at csaeger@hotmail.com.

Jamie Sarfeh lives with her parents and older sister. She will be a college freshman next fall, where she plans to study biology and international relations. Jamie is a lover of the arts and spends much of her time painting and writing. She is also an avid tennis player.

Emily Scavarda is an undergraduate. She enjoys studio art classes, is majoring in chemistry, and doesn't run as often as she would like to. She also enjoys surfing when she goes back to Southern California in the summers. E-mail her at silveraquareus@yahoo.com.

Annabel Murphy Schizas is currently attending college to earn her degree in business administration with a concentration in marketing. She is interested in fashion design and plans to attend design school once she graduates. She currently lives in the south with her husband.

Mike Shapiro's cartoons appear in many publications including the *Wall Street Journal, Barron's*, the *Harvard Business Review*, and *Reader's Digest*. He is also a contributor to many legal, medical, and business journals and has done work for animation studios as well as advertising agencies. In addition to the above, Mike frequently draws caricatures at live events. Mike lives in Washington, DC, with his wife, Amy, their son, Jake, and their two noisy dogs.

Jason Sherwood has been published in numerous literary journals and anthologies, including *Teen Ink, The Magnolia Quarterly, Wordsmith's Magazine*, and *National High School Poetry Anthology*, and has received writing awards from the Gulf Coast Writer's Association, the Live Poet's Society, Bergen Community College, the National Council of Teachers of English, and the Hamilton Press, to name a few. He published his debut novel, *Wilting*, at age sixteen, which is available online from Amazon and Barnes and Noble.

Aaron Shield received his bachelor of arts and his master of arts. He expects to receive his Ph.D. in linguistics. He is currently conducting research on autistic children's communicative development.

Renata Silberblatt graduated with honors majoring in English literature. She currently resides in California, where she works for an environmental nonprofit.

Stephanie Skaluba has previously published poetry, fiction, and nonfiction works. She is a licensed nurse at a long-term care facility. She is a voracious reader, avid concert goer, and terrible dancer. Feel free to e-mail her at ska_11th@yahoo.com.

Adam Smith is a junior in high school. He lettered in swimming and track and also works as a lifeguard at the community YMCA. Adam enjoys show choir, debate, and student government. However, his favorite activity continues to be going to school dances with his girlfriend of two years.

Jessie Spellman is currently attending college in the northeast. She plans to enter politics and enjoys reading, writing, going to the beach, shopping, and exercising.

At the age of sixteen, **Ashley Strickler** has several published works to her credit, including her first novel, *Once Upon a Time*. Ashley, a high-school sophomore, enjoys reading, writing, spending time with her companion, and her quiet life in Texas. E-mail her at rajanitzu@yahoo.com.

Kaidi Stroud received her bachelor of arts. She currently teaches at a Montessori preschool in Idaho. She is also a raft guide, avid runner, skiier, and backpacker. She will be a Mrs. Kaidi in June 2007 and begin a master's in English and education in the fall. She may be contacted at Kaidistroud@hotmail.com.

Bonnie Tamarin majored in journalism in college after developing a love for writing in childhood and high school. Currently, Bonnie works in clinical research where she continues to apply her writing skills to the medical field.

Based in the United Kingdom, **Paul Taylor** is a popular cartoonist in European and American magazines.

Jill Telford is working toward her bachelor of arts degree in English. She is also working on a novel inspired by her life. She likes traveling, kayaking, painting, and photography. For more information, please e-mail her at jill.telford@gmail.com.

Suzanne Timmons received her bachelor of arts in elementary education and lives in Massachusetts.

Andrew Toos has established a national reputation through his offbeat lifestyle cartoons for clients such as *Reader's Digest, Saturday Evening Post, Gallery, Stern, Accountancy, Baseball Digest, Ceo, Washington Post, Barron's, Bayer Corp, Good Housekeeping, Cosmopolitan,* and many other titles and media outlets. His work is licensed through CartoonResource.com. Andrew lives with his wife, Nancy, in Florida.

Dominick Vargas received his bachelor of arts in English. He currently teaches at a college and plans on continuing his education. Dominick loves reading, writing, sports, and especially traveling. He can be reached at dom.vargas@gmail.com.

Ann Virgo is currently attending college and enjoys leadership and free writing for inspiration and vision. She loves staying involved and has future aspirations to go into nonprofit business. Her goal is to touch the lives of others through her work.

Katie Weiss graduated with a bachelor's in environmental science. She is now pursuing a master's in education. She enjoys nature and outdoor pursuits including backpacking, rock climbing, and skiing.

Julie White wrote about her brother's battle with cancer when she was in high school. She has since earned her bachelor of arts with honors. Julie works at a hospital and plans to earn her master's degree in art therapy, enabling her to embrace her two passions: art and helping children find happiness and healing. She loves to write and inspire others. Please e-mail her at julicannabellewhite@yahoo.com.

Kimberly Williams is pursuing her bachelor of science in art history and is a previous California runner-up in the Voice of Democracy Essay Contest. She enjoys dancing, skiing, playing ultimate Frisbee, writing, and attending arts performances.

Megan Willman is currently alive and kickin' as a senior in high school. She enjoys reading and writing as well as spending time with her friends and family. Her piece "Visiting Hours Are Over" is dedicated to the memory of her grandmother, Rose.

Stephanie Rose Xavier is a college freshman concentrating on animal science with a minor in creative writing. She hopes to one day make traveling her hobby and see all the places she dreamed of as a child. Stephanie loves animals and, at times, considers them more stimulating, affectionate, and thoughtful than most humans! Her boyfriend has been a true supporter of her writing and pushes her every day to write more and more.

Annie Xu is a senior in college, expecting to graduate in 2007.

Jeff Yao is currently a high school student. He enjoys swimming, debating, and watching movies. He has a nineteen-year-old sister named Grace and a toy poodle (as in the breed, not a plush) named Dooby, who likes to play with tissues. He wants to attend the Air Force Academy and looks forward to someday becoming a commercial airline pilot.

Katie Zbydniewski is currently attending college pursuing a bachelor's degree in English. Katie enjoys listening to music, swimming, and reading. Please e-mail her at katiegc24@yahoo.com.

V. L. Laurense Zinger is currently a third-year English student in college. She loves to read and write, as it is a wonderful stress reliever and a great way to express herself. She hopes to eventually work in the editing and/or publishing industry and to write several books of her own.